ISSUE 5, FEBRUARY 2019

AUSTRALIAN FOREIGN AFFAIRS

Contributors

Aarti Betigeri is a journalist who writes regularly on South Asian issues.

Santilla Chingaipe is a journalist who has reported on Africa and Australia's African communities.

Peter Fray is co-director of the Centre for Media Transition at University Technology Sydney and founder of PolitiFact Australia.

Sam Geall is executive editor at *China Dialogue* and associate fellow at Chatham House, a think tank in London.

Linda Jaivin is a novelist, essayist, translator and cultural commentator with a long-standing interest in China.

George Megalogenis is a journalist, political commentator and author.

Sam Roggeveen is director of the International Security Program at the Lowy Institute and founding editor of *The Interpreter* website.

Sarah Teo is an associate research fellow at the S. Rajaratnam School of International Studies in Singapore.

Christos Tsiolkas is a novelist, playwright and essayist.

David Walker is a historian and emeritus professor at Deakin University whose latest book is *Stranded Nation: White Australia in an Asian Region*.

Australian Foreign Affairs is published three times a year by Schwartz Publishing Pty Ltd. Publisher: Morry Schwartz. ISBN 978-1-76064-1009 ISSN 2208-5912 ALL RIGHTS RESERVED. No part of this publication may be reproduced, stored in a retrieval system, or transmitted in any form by any means, electronic, mechanical, photocopying, recording or otherwise, without the prior consent of the publishers. Essays, reviews and correspondence © retained by the authors. Subscriptions – 1 year print & digital auto-renew (3 issues): $49.99 within Australia incl. GST. 1 year print and digital subscription (3 issues): $59.99 within Australia incl. GST. 2 year print & digital (6 issues): $114.99 within Australia incl. GST. 1 year digital only auto-renew: $29.99. Payment may be made by MasterCard, Visa or Amex, or by cheque made out to Schwartz Publishing Pty Ltd. Payment includes postage and handling. To subscribe, fill out the form inside this issue, subscribe online at www.australianforeignaffairs.com, email subscribe@australianforeignaffairs.com or phone 1800 077 514 / 61 3 9486 0288. Correspondence should be addressed to: The Editor, Australian Foreign Affairs, Level 1, 221 Drummond Street, Carlton VIC 3053 Australia Phone: 61 3 9486 0288 Email: enquiries@australianforeignaffairs.com Editor: Jonathan Pearlman. Associate Editor: Chris Feik. Consulting Editor: Allan Gyngell. Deputy Editor: Julia Carlomagno. Editorial intern: Ebony Young. Management: Caitlin Yates. Marketing: Elisabeth Young, Georgia Mill and Iryna Byelyayeva. Publicity: Anna Lensky. Design: Peter Long. Production Coordination: Marilyn de Castro. Typesetting: Akiko Chan. Cover photo of Scott Morrison and international world leaders © Dita Alangkara/ AAP. Printed in Australia by McPherson's Printing Group.

ARE WE ASIAN YET?

When the debate about Australia's place in Asia last flared, in the 1990s, John Howard famously declared that Australia did not have to choose "between our history and our geography".

He was right. Australia is the product of its history – its unreconciled relationship with its first peoples, its British past, its turn towards the United States – and its geography, as a continent at the southern edge of Asia. These two forces shape the nation – and they leave it with very few choices.

The extent to which Australia is Asian or Western is a question, rather than a choice. But answering it, and describing the nation's evolving identity, is not equivalent to, as Howard claimed, "disowning the past". Instead, it is an inquiry that reveals much about Australia's character, outlook, and place and reputation in the region and the world.

In the twenty-four years since Howard's declaration, changes in Australia all appear to be tilting it away from the West and towards

Asia. Today, Asian countries account for eleven of Australia's top fifteen trading partners, and at least 56 per cent of Australia's migrant intake. Canberra's diplomatic and defence ties across the region have deepened, and Australia is increasingly accepted as a participant of regional groupings such as the East Asian Summit or, from 2022, the Asian Games.

Clearly, the benefits that Australia receives from its geography are increasing. But the benefits from its history appear to be shrinking. Australia's Western heritage led it to align with the two great powers of the previous two centuries, first Britain and then the United States. Now the regional balance is changing, and the United States' relative power in Asia is in decline. For Australia, being a Western outpost in Asia will soon lose its allure. The emphasis will no longer fall on "Western" but on "outpost".

Yet much of Australia's cultural and political life and global outlook stem from Western institutions. And its growing reach into the region is often transactional, which may limit the extent of its engagement. Australia may find its prosperity and security in Asia, but its people, politics, location and economy will mix in ways that are impossible to predict.

As Australia tries to make the most of the Asian Century, its place in Asia is likely to remain an open question.

Jonathan Pearlman

SIGNIFICANT OTHER

Anxieties about
Australia's Asian future

David Walker

In 1968, the University of New South Wales (UNSW) chose the topic "Australia: A Part of Asia?" for its annual symposium. The university's professor of history, Frank Crowley, initially knocked back the invitation to speak, declaring in no uncertain terms that Australia never had been and never would be part of Asia. When prevailed upon to take part, he maintained that Australia was an "outpost of Europe". While he saw value in Asian studies, he did not think Australia should move closer to Asia politically or liberalise its immigration policy. All speakers at the symposium stressed the importance of Australia's European heritage. None considered Australia part of Asia.

In 1992, Prime Minister Paul Keating delivered an address, "Australia and Asia: Knowing Who We Are", in which he referenced Robert Menzies' early speeches celebrating Australia's place in the

British Empire. In the 1930s, wool exports to Japan had grown, speeding Australia's recovery from the Great Depression and encouraging speculation that the nation's economic future lay in Asia. Despite such opportunities, Menzies insisted that Australians would always put their "blood ties" with Britain before commerce. In contrast, Keating wanted to establish Australia's "rightful presence" in the Asia-Pacific. He was concerned that "the ghost of Empire", faded and diminished as it had become, still stood in the way of the cultural changes needed to promote Asian engagement. He insisted that if Australia did not succeed in forging ties in Asia, it would not succeed anywhere.

For Julie Bishop, Minister for Foreign Affairs and Trade in the Coalition government until August 2018, the New Colombo Plan became a personal enthusiasm and a key to Asian engagement. She often alluded to the proud antecedents of this scheme, a reminder that Coalition governments had taken Australia's place in Asia seriously. The original Colombo Plan had been a great success for Percy Spender, Menzies' Minister for External Affairs. In discussing the New Colombo Plan, Bishop kept her language pragmatic and emphasised economic diplomacy. Australia's national interest was best served, Bishop maintained, by encouraging Asian prosperity.

In this protracted discussion of identity and place, the ground is constantly shifting.

Asian futures

One of Australia's defining characteristics is the belief – sometimes clouded by fear, sometimes bedazzled by expectation of oriental riches – that the nation is headed for an Asian future. Destiny allows little room for choice. Despite their attachments to Britain, Australian settlers gradually discovered that their continent's geography and hot climate was perhaps better suited to Asian than European settlement. In the decade after federation, Australia was a nation adrift, caught between a receding Europe and a rapidly advancing Asia. Concern about this apparent dilemma persisted for many decades. It is still present in 2019.

Asia dreaming has been a recurring theme in the national narrative

Australia's attempts to imagine "Asia" reveal a number of recurrent anxieties: concerns about racial identity, fear of invasion, how to survive and prosper in a non-Western neighbourhood, and the impact of immigrants on the national character.

First, what is "Asia"? It is a shifting idea, defined by the time and circumstance in which it is discussed or envisioned, rather than by geography. The reality of Asia is rather different from this imagining, encompassing a diversity of cultures, languages, religions and histories. At the UNSW symposium, this was emphasised by Sibnarayan Ray, head of Indian Studies at the University of Melbourne, who reminded his Australian audience that "Asia is not one". He urged his listeners to acknowledge that its people are Chinese, Indian or Indonesian, "but they are hardly Asians".

Our home-grown writings on imagined Asia typically tell us more about Australia and its cultural and political preoccupations and anxieties than about any specific Asian society. Yet while "Asia" was and is a fluid idea, it nonetheless has a remarkably stable location in time: Asia is always the future. For instance, in October 2012, when Prime Minister Julia Gillard introduced the 314-page "Australia in the Asian Century" White Paper, she twice used the phrase "we have not been here before", reinforcing her message with reference to the "new China" and the "new India" and describing the world Australia faced in Asia as "unprecedented". Not so fast. If we look back at the history, Asia dreaming has been a recurring theme in the national narrative.

There are two problems with a mindset fixated on the future. First, Asia is always unfamiliar territory, new and unsettling. Each generation deludes itself that it is the first to face a rising Asia. "Knowing Asia" becomes a project for visionaries who have no time and certainly no need for history. Second, by casting Asia as the future, we fail to understand that the Asia we imagine is a product of our popular culture and national history, with an uncertain basis in reality.

Eurasian possibilities

Let us take a brief look at the history of Australia's varied "Asian futures", beginning with the long-running divide over whether the nation's racial and ethnic character is, or should be, Western or Asian, or some mixture of the two.

There are earlier starting points, but we can begin in 1829 with Edward Gibbon Wakefield, an advocate of migration to the colonies. In his famous *A Letter from Sydney, the Principal Town of Australasia*, Wakefield derided the idea that Australia was a lonely, isolated continent. Rather than being "out of the way", Australia had Asia on its very doorstep, with opportunities for frequent interaction with a great diversity of nations, cultures and economies. Wakefield promoted Chinese immigration, believing that the Chinese people's impressive skills could turn Australia's "wilderness" into a productive garden.

In 1888, congregational minister Reverend James Jefferis offered a more expansive multiracial vision of Australia's future. He imagined how Chinese, Japanese and Indian settlers could contribute to a glorious new Australia. Each would bring distinctive attributes – the Chinese would be hardworking, the Japanese artistic and the Indians spiritual: "Australia will become great by a fusion and mingling of races ... East and West will join hands."

Jefferis' union of East and West ran counter to powerful calls for a white Australia that celebrated racial homogeneity as the country's highest ideal and likeliest future. Even so, racial mixing appealed to a range of commentators as the way forward. In the 1850s, *Blackwood's Magazine* prophesied that a new "golden race" would emerge from the goldfields. Later, *The Sydney Morning Herald* argued that an infusion of Chinese blood would prevent white settlers from degenerating into a "soft" and "spongy" race in Australia's hot climate. The historical debate shows us that Australia was never thought of as either wholly European or completely Asian.

From the 1920s, as genetic research made the case for "hybrid vigour", University of Sydney geographer Griffith Taylor wondered how, without racial mixing, his Australian grandchildren would fare when China became a world power. He became very unpopular among White Australia enthusiasts by suggesting that most Australian climates were ill-suited for European settlement. His widely publicised maps showed how Townsville, Brisbane and Sydney shared "homoclines" with Calcutta, Hong Kong and Shanghai. Only Hobart had a true English climate.

In 1949, the demographer W.D. Borrie predicted that Australia would soon be peopled by a "new Eurasian stock". Bishop Burgmann, an Anglican social critic, loved the idea; such people would have the fine natural colour that white Australians "seek to attain on the beaches". Although racial mixing was an outcome feared by the nation's first Minister for Immigration, Labor's Arthur Calwell – a White Australia stalwart – the Eurasian ideal nevertheless proved remarkably tenacious. In 1983, Bill Hayden, Labor's Minister for Foreign Affairs, welcomed Australia's probable Eurasian future. Later, Prime Minister Keating declared that Australia would become "the world's first Eurasian nation". Even the conservative historian and proud contrarian John Hirst imagined future Australians as "beautiful" honey-coloured people.

In 2017, in the first issue of this journal, political commentator George Megalogenis called for Australia to become a Eurasian nation, in line with increasing Asian migration. Yet a "Eurasian future" looks very like the last gasp of an older, thoroughly racialised argument. Why would coming generations think of themselves as genetically or racially Eurasian rather than as Australians of Asian heritage or, more simply, as Australians?

The Eurasian ideal was always seen as European/Asian, never as black/white, which was unacceptable to race theorists. Visions of a Eurasian future routinely excluded Indigenous Australians. But there can be no convincing Australian future that does not recognise the history, cultures and creativity of Indigenous Australia.

An imagined Asia was posited as a deadly threat to White Australia

Asian invasion

While Keating invoked the "ghost of Empire" as an impediment to Australia finding its place in Asia, another even more venerable spectre haunts this discussion: the prospect of an invasive Asia plotting the downfall of a vulnerable White Australia. This ghost has frightened people since before Federation.

In the 1880s, William Lane, a labour movement organiser, intellectual and journalist, was appalled by the prospect of a mixed-race

Australia. In *White or Yellow? A Story of the Race War of A.D. 1908*, he laid out his own centenary vision with Australia's first story of Asian invasion. In this novella, race war engulfs Queensland. China emerges as the cruel destroyer of Australia's youthful promise. The reader learns that the racial enemy is emboldened to strike because sections of the community have chosen to collaborate with the Chinese in commerce and politics. The rising generation pays a terrible price for the naivety of their elders, who believed that the Chinese were just harmless "celestials".

Lane's tale is a critical departure in futurist speculation. Invasion shifted the possible impact of rising Asia from the realm of generalised abstraction. His story is full of local Queensland references, recognisable people and familiar landmarks. At its core is the survivalist binary of "them" and "us", made clear by the title, *White or Yellow?* Further tales of Asian invasion were to follow from other Australian writers.

Who were these Asian enemies? With the Dutch in control of the Netherlands East Indies (now Indonesia), and the British ruling India, the focus of concern was East Asia. Whether it was Japan or China or a combination of their forces ("the yellow peril"), an imagined Asia was posited as a deadly threat to White Australia. This terrible prospect ensured that defence and border security became top priorities for all political parties.

While military hardware was important, so too were the qualities a supposedly vulnerable nation would need in a race war. Australia was already a precociously urban society. Doubts were raised about whether suburban weaklings would have the grit to defend the nation. Commentators looked beyond the cities and saw in the bushman a figure who held the key to White Australia's survival. Virile men who could handle horses, guns and hardship were the race patriots Australia would need in the coming conflict.

The nation's bush bard, Henry Lawson, had a lot to say about this. A persistent geopolitical imaginary informs much of his verse. In "To Be Amused" (1906), a poem about an Asian invasion, he celebrates the "Bushmen" who fight and die defending this "outpost of the white man's race". In "Song of Australia" (1908), Lawson calls upon Australia's poets, singers and statesmen to let Europe know that youthful Australia represents a new dawn for the white race.

Invasion stories spelt out an inexorable logic: just as white had replaced black, so too would yellow, in the language of the day, replace white. The genre was heavily concerned with nation-building, weighing up national strengths and limitations and the masculine qualities required for war with Asia. The menace of rising Asia put paid to Australia's growing republican sentiments and strengthened appeals to the blood ties that so enamoured Robert Menzies.

Australians of the early twentieth century did not inherently fear Asians. This worldview was instilled through repeated and carefully crafted messages. Given that Australia was a nation of port cities, which are well known for their cosmopolitan acceptance of difference, the task of shutting Asia out demanded constant vigilance. Curiosity about Asia had to be dismissed as deluded and possibly treacherous, a sign of disloyalty.

There were recalcitrants, and these were often women. One rebel was the prolific novelist Rosa Campbell Praed. In *Madame Izan* (1899), she satirised Australia's growing enthusiasm for the bushman as an indispensable saviour. Her blind heroine chooses a cultivated Japanese suitor over a pastoralist from Queensland, a muscular exponent of yellow-peril warnings. In setting her story in Japan, Praed picked the Asian nation that most troubled and beguiled post-Federation Australia.

Invasion stories still play a role in Australia's view of Asia. Some are spawned locally, and others are imported from America. As Pauline Hanson warned that Australia was about to be "swamped by Asians" in her maiden parliamentary speech, airport novels by prolific American writers described the horrific consequences of Chinese invasion. Clive Cussler's *Flood Tide* (1997), Stephen J. Cannell's *Riding the Snake* (1998) and Tom Clancy's door-stopper *The Bear and the Dragon* (2000) spoke of primal forces, sinister oriental adversaries, porous borders and looming national decline. Their snakes, floods and dragons are the stock in trade for survivalists. More recently, Keith McArdle maintained the genre with *The Reckoning: The Day Australia Fell* (2013), as did American writer James Wesley, Rawles in *Expatriates: A Novel of the Coming Global Collapse* (2013), where Australia faces a threat from radical Islamic forces in Indonesia.

While claiming to be a strictly factual account of recent Chinese influence in Australia, Clive Hamilton's *Silent Invasion* (2018) draws upon and fans many of the anxieties of invasion narratives. Hamilton argues that most Australian institutions, including universities and state and federal political parties, are "being penetrated and shaped by a complex system of influence and control overseen by agencies serving the Chinese Communist Party". While the Chinese government maintains a close and at times problematic interest in Australia's affairs, Hamilton's claim exaggerates the reality. Such fears of malign external influence seem to be an Australian constant, deeply rooted in popular culture. These ideas have attracted many novelists, poets, journalists and commentators, yet foreign policy debates rarely enter this troubling territory.

When Asian economies were booming, Australia wanted to be Asian

————————————

Nevertheless, speculative writing on the geopolitics of Australian belonging has much to say about who we are and the nation we have wanted to become.

Surviving in Asia

Beyond invasion fears, geography raised another question: how would White Australia hope to survive and prosper in an Asian region? In the 1960s Britain, with American encouragement, disengaged from Asia and moved towards Europe. The Asian world had become a complex and troubling mix of decolonised nations, suspicious of the retreating old white world and susceptible to communism. Australia needed to engage quickly with Asia to win trading and Cold War partners. The White Australia policy, sold for more than half a century as the sacred foundation of the nation, was no help. Australia had to extract itself from racist rhetoric, and fashion a new language of tolerance.

Enter "neighbourliness". The Department of External Affairs hoped that Australia, if marketed as Asia's newest and friendliest neighbour, could win supporters in the region while buying more time to increase its population through post-war European immigration. Keeping Asia out had not changed, but putting on a friendly face while doing so was new.

The desire to demonstrate that Australia was an Asia-friendly nation became a post-war imperative. Government programs were introduced to make Asians see Australia more positively: Radio Australia beamed its cheerful messages north; Colombo Plan students were told that Australians had no racial prejudices. Asian visitors were carted around arid regions to demonstrate that Australia was terribly dry – it was surely an act of kindness to warn our neighbours against settling somewhere so hot and horrible.

Australia's move towards Asia was bound to be difficult, given the many powerful stories told about the dangerous "near North". Yet engagement proved easier to defend as expanding Asian markets eased the pain of withdrawal from a shrinking British trading world. From the late 1950s, trade with East Asia proved critical to the Australian economy. Many of the spoils flowed to rural communities that might otherwise have resisted such momentous change. By 1971, 570 branches of the Country Party favoured recognition of China; only thirteen were opposed.

Yet change did not come without difficult questions. From the 1950s, the Department of External Affairs worried that its phrase "part of Asia", used in its dealings across Asia as proof of friendliness, had developed an unwelcome life in the wider Australian culture. The words invited questions about the damage done to Australia's reputation in Asia by an immigration policy that did not appear to be altogether neighbourly. Pressures for immigration reform mounted. Being "part of Asia" became a rallying cry for noisy progressives impatient for change.

It was one thing for Australia to announce that it was part of Asia, but quite another for its neighbours to agree. During the UNSW symposium, Wang Gungwu, Professor of Far Eastern history at the Australian National University, asked "part of Asia for whom?" He confessed that he had never met an Asian who considered Australia part of Asia and did not believe he ever would.

In the 1990s, Malaysian prime minister Mahathir Mohamad was scornful of Keating's push to have Australia accepted as part of Asia. He noted sceptically that when Britain ruled the waves, Australia wanted to be British. When the United States rose to power after World War II, Australians jumped into bed with the Americans, and when Asian economies were booming, Australia wanted to be Asian. Now back in power, Mahathir has not changed his views. Recently, responding to Indonesian suggestions that Australia could join the ten-nation regional organisation ASEAN, he noted that Australia still needed to show it was more "Asian than European". To him, "it sticks out like a sore thumb" as an outpost of Europe.

Early in 2018, I taught an MA class at Beijing Foreign Studies University examining Australian responses to Asia. When I put it to my Chinese students that Australia should be thought of as "part of Asia", they greeted the proposal with a mixture of astonishment and polite scepticism.

We are one, but we are many

In the last fifty years, the number of Asian immigrants entering Australia has increased dramatically. George Megalogenis' analysis of ABS census data from 2016 indicates an "Australia of genuine diversity", with 28 per cent of the population born overseas, more than a third of these from Asia. The mix of communities, their relations to homeland and host country, and their histories of immigration constitute a uniquely Australian pattern of mixing, mingling and settling. Their complex stories are neatly captured in the SBS program *Where Are You Really From?*, where comedian Michael Hing, whose family has been in Australia for more than a century, speaks to Chinese, Sikh and South Sudanese migrants. They tease out, often in broad Australian accents, their transnational backgrounds and identifications.

Australians like these stories celebrating the nation's striking diversity. Yet the white-settler narrative, dominant for so long, has not entirely lost its voice. It can be heard in Macca's *Australia All Over* on ABC Radio every Sunday morning, a wistful evocation of the old days and the old ways, of the authenticity of the bush and the falsity of the city and those out-of-touch politicians.

Some white citizens are fearful of the loss of this supposedly more authentic Australia. Others are attracted by the messages of Pauline Hanson's One Nation party, worried at being "swamped by Asians" or threatened by Muslims. In October 2018, Hanson created a furore in the Australian Senate when she used white supremacist language in a motion declaring that it is "OK to be white". Although the motion was narrowly defeated (31 to 28), a confused Coalition had joined Hanson, a stance it later called "regrettable". Such claims about anti-white discrimination are a fringe issue, but the fringe is becoming noisier, with renewed political influence.

> **To Howard, it was "self-evident" that Australia was an "outpost of Western civilisation"**

Some in modern Australia also have anxieties over the fate of our European heritage. They circle the wagons, calling for the education system to uphold what they see as a besieged Western canon. Their calls to Westernise our education system raise questions not unlike those posed by calls for a more Asia-literate curriculum. What aspects of the West should be studied? What aspects of Asia? And what of the crossovers? Where would we put the French-born

Chinese-American cellist Yo-Yo Ma? If the cello goes West and Ma goes East, the music stops.

The politics of "Asia"

Through the 1990s, the question of which of the two major parties was best placed to work effectively with Asia came to the fore, sharpened by Keating's insistence that the forelock-tugging heirs of the Menzies tradition facing him in parliament were not up to the task. Under Bob Hawke and Paul Keating, Labor presented itself as the only party with a bold vision for Australia's Asian future. On becoming prime minister in 1983, Hawke insisted that "our future lies in enmeshment" with Asia. In 1988, he embraced the idea of Asia literacy, in parallel with economic reforms – floating the dollar, reducing tariffs, promoting exports to Asia – designed to secure Australia's place as a legitimate Asia-Pacific power.

Keating wanted a more systematic engagement with Asia, rather than enmeshment. He foresaw a time when more Australians spoke Asian languages and understood Asian cultures, where business-people familiar with the Asia-Pacific valued Australians of Asian heritage. Our national culture would influence but also be shaped by our Asian neighbours. Keating's well-known formulation was that Australia would seek its security *in* but not *from* Asia. For Keating, engagement did not mean, as some critics implied, making Australia more Asian, but making Australia more Australian, "sure of who we are and what we stand for". He saw an Asia-literate Australia severing its ties to the monarchy and becoming a republic.

Labor's ambition led to the creation of a new "regional architecture". Hawke and Keating laid the groundwork for an intergovern-
mental forum for Pacific Rim economies. November 1989 saw the first
Asia-Pacific Economic Cooperation (APEC) meeting in Canberra,
chaired by Labor's Minister for Foreign Affairs, Gareth Evans. In 1994,
APEC adopted the Bogor Goals to advance free trade and investment
across the Asia-Pacific. Evans had earlier played a pivotal role in the
development of the Paris Peace Accords that led to the end of the war
in Cambodia.

Some Australians were apprehensive about Keating's vision of
Australia growing closer to Asia. On becoming prime minister in
1996, John Howard shifted the emphasis. He strengthened ties with
London and Washington. Turning to Asia, he focused on the rapidly
growing middle class, with its pleasing appetite for the goods, services
and resources that Australia was so well-placed to provide. Howard
distanced middle-class Asia from the overcrowded, invasive Asia of
recent memory. It was reassuring to be told that middle-class Asia
preferred refrigerators to revenge or revolution.

In a lecture to the Griffith Asia Institute in 2016, Howard
explained that middle-class Asia was of "colossal ongoing significance" to Australia. However, echoing Menzies, he maintained that
"common values would always trump trade links". Australia would
always remain closer to the United States than to China. To Howard,
it was "self-evident" that Australia was an "outpost of Western civilisation"; thinking of Australia as an Asian nation was "pointless and

futile". When in office, he used Anzac Day ceremonies, not least at Gallipoli, to reinforce the message that the Australian nation had been forged in war by the bushman soldier. Australians needed to "respect and cherish what we have distinctively achieved". As the nation's longest-serving prime minister since Menzies, Howard's scepticism about Australia's status as an Asian country carried weight. But did he protest too much?

Where Howard avoided heady rhetoric about Australia's Asian destiny, Kevin Rudd was altogether more enthusiastic. In 2008, as Australia's first Mandarin-speaking prime minister, he urged Australians to "go Asian". His Australia would become "the most Asia-literate country in the collective West". Yet two years on, *The Sydney Morning Herald* noted that the study of Asian languages had "sunk to new lows" in Australian schools. Ten years later, deputy Opposition leader Tanya Plibersek found that progress had "stagnated". She promised that an incoming Shorten government would revive Asian-language teaching.

Prime Minister Julia Gillard sought a strong Asian focus by commissioning the "Australia in the Asian Century" White Paper. She called for a "more Asia-literate and Asia-capable nation" by 2025. Within weeks of coming to power in 2013, Prime Minister Tony Abbott archived Gillard's big-picture White Paper. He turned away from developing Asia literacy, revived imperial honours and talked up the "Anglosphere". The focus shifted back to trade. In 2014, Abbott led the largest-ever business delegation to the Asian region, and Minister for Trade and Investment Andrew Robb negotiated free trade agreements with South Korea, Japan and China.

Under Abbott and his successors, Malcolm Turnbull and Scott Morrison, "economic diplomacy" has taken precedence over cultural diplomacy. The Asian threat – more particularly the China threat – has returned. In his response to Asia, Turnbull began at the optimistic pole of Asian engagement, stressing the rewards that would flow from a confidently outward-looking and innovative approach to the region. He soon shifted to tougher talk about vulnerable borders, terrorist threats and regional instability, an emphasis supported by Morrison and Home Affairs minister Peter Dutton. That said, no government dares to put Australia's trading relationship with China at risk. As a new prime minister, and coming from a marketing background, Morrison insists that "Australia and China can get on with business as usual", emphasising the value of the Chinese as "customers".

With the rise of Asia, Western prestige and self-regard may decline

Changes at the top have resulted in confusing shifts in the terminology describing Asia. Robert Menzies began his prime ministership extolling Australia's potential leadership role as a "Pacific" nation. For a time, the term "Pacific Rim" found favour, while from the 1970s, discussion turned to Australia's role in the "Asia-Pacific". Gareth Evans also spoke of the "East Asian hemisphere". In some quarters,

"Asia-Pacific" has now lost its "Asia" prefix, to re-emerge as "Indo-Pacific". At the 2018 APEC conference in Papua New Guinea, China's President Xi spoke of the "Asia-Pacific" while US Vice President Mike Pence used the term "Indo-Pacific", implying different understandings of the region. Both major parties have renewed talk of the Pacific, the "blue continent" – no longer the Pacific of Menzies, but referring to the island nations of the Pacific Ocean.

Are we Asian yet?

In 1909, a short story appeared in the glossy magazine *Australia To-day*. Australia was a new and untried federation, far removed from the protection of Britain's powerful navy. Many thought the continent was dangerously "empty", a tempting prize in an overcrowded part of the world.

The story opens with Sydneysiders flocking to hear an important public lecture by a distinguished British journalist who has just completed a fact-finding tour of the new nation. The visitor tells his listeners about a dream that transported him into the future, to the Australia of 1959.

The journalist's vision is wonderfully reassuring. Australia's cities have blossomed into flourishing ports, crowded with shipping from all corners of the world. What about the formidable challenge of the "empty" interior? Even better news. Vigorous settlements and prosperous farms are spread across the length and breadth of Australia.

But the visitor has one more revelation. During his dream, he did not see a single white face. Shock horror! Australia's remarkable transformation is an Asian, not an Anglo, accomplishment. His message is clear: to get things really humming, Australia needs an Asian makeover.

The clever little story forms part of the continuing body of speculative thinking about Australia's Asian futures. From the outset, settler Australia had an uncertain hold on its strange continent. Unwilling to learn from Indigenous Australians, and uneasy about their "tainted" convict heritage, the settlers looked to the future. Anxieties about the nation's identity continue to shape its speculative thinking.

Three of the words in the question "are we Asian yet?" are rather tricky. Who are "we"? What constitutes "Asian"? And when is "yet"? Recently, the conservative commentator Andrew Bolt complained that there was no longer any "we" – "we" had become "them". Bolt found the proof he needed in Melbourne's Box Hill, which he declared had become Chinese. Although only a third of Box Hill's population is Chinese by birth or background, Bolt doubled this figure.

Who are these Chinese? There is no simple answer. They may come from the south or north of mainland China, or from Taiwan, Hong Kong, Malaysia, Singapore or Vietnam. They may be Australian-born. The diversity of the populations now living here will in years to come have a strong impact on how we see Asia. What will "Asia" mean to Australia over the next 100 years? Australia came to nationhood as a settler society during a period of Western economic, political and cultural dominance. We saw Asia as an inferior collection of defeated or stagnant civilisations. Our voices still carry the authority of this historically significant but relatively short-lived European dominance, when the West formed a high opinion of itself racially, culturally and politically. But economic power is now shifting back to the Asian region. Asian nations are on course to regain a position approximating the world of the mid-eighteenth century, when two-thirds of global economic activity centred on China and India. What will this mean for cultural power?

While there is no automatic correlation between economic power and cultural power, there can be little doubt that as Asia grows, so too will the influence of Asian – and in particular Chinese – cultures, practices and norms. While it is pertinent for Australians to appreciate the buying power of the growing Asian middle class, it will become even more important to understand the cultural logic of their purchasing practices. To do this, we will have to get closer and come to know them as people, not just as "customers".

With the rise of Asia, Western prestige and self-regard may decline at every level. The status of "whites" will be much discussed. Middle-power nations such as Australia may handle this transition rather better than the United States, which has more cultural capital to lose and more sensitivity about its threatened global ranking.

We need to address any hesitancy in Australia about becoming "part of Asia" by directing more attention to how we form our views about other societies. We need to understand how Asia has been represented in Australia over the past two centuries and what that past now means to us. Perhaps we should spend less time gazing anxiously into the unknowable future and more time examining the knowable past. That might teach us something about the problematic nature of cultural assumptions, and something about ourselves as well. Only then will we – an English-speaking, European-colonised, culturally diverse southern continent – know where we stand. ∎

RED DETACHMENT

Is Chinese culture
beyond reach?

Linda Jaivin

In February 2017, everything that is difficult about cultural engagement with the People's Republic of China (PRC) was on display inside and out of the Arts Centre Melbourne. The National Ballet of China, at the invitation of the new Asia-Pacific Triennial of Performing Arts (AsiaTOPA), was staging *The Red Detachment of Women*. The ballet tells the story of a poor peasant girl who is saved from the clutches of a despotic landowner by the Chinese Red Army in the 1930s. She joins the women's military corps and returns with them to heroically defeat and kill the landowner and his allies. With its epic themes of victimhood and revenge, and its cast of gravity-defying, rifle-toting, flag-flying, stern-faced ballerinas, *The Red Detachment of Women* is a song-and-dance spectacle of a scale and type rarely seen on the Australian stage.

But just how do we "see" it? The ballet is also a work of unabashed propaganda about a violent period in modern Chinese history, told in unambiguous terms, with clear heroes and villains. It was inspired by a true story – but there are other true stories, too. My friend Hou Dejian's grandmother owned a small amount of land in a remote Sichuan village. During Land Reform, the revolutionaries wrapped her hands in cotton and set them alight, crippling her for life. Visiting the village half a century later, I was taken aback to see just how modest was the house she'd lived in, how few were her fields. Certainly, there were greedy, cruel and exploitative rural overlords who badly abused the landless farmers who relied on them. But propaganda permits no shades of grey, no universal notion of humanity, no empathy.

In Chinese, "propaganda", *xuanchuan*, literally means "proclaim and circulate". Propaganda plays a central role in both governance and cultural production in the PRC: as of 2018, Chinese media, publishing, radio, television and film all answer to the Department of Propaganda; the department answers to the Communist Party's Central Committee. Not all mainland Chinese art is propaganda – not by far, even if the Party would like it to be. But *The Red Detachment of Women* most definitely is. It was one of the prime entertainments of the Cultural Revolution – a movement launched in 1966 by Mao to purge his enemies within the Party and realise his radical, totalitarian-left vision for China. During the Cultural Revolution, millions of people, including many well-loved cultural figures, were detained, beaten, tortured, killed or driven to suicide, and youthful Red Guards, spurred on by Mao, trashed much of China's ancient material cultural heritage.

Male friends who came of age during that sexually repressive decade tell me they loved *The Red Detachment*'s brand of revolutionary cheesecake: hot soldier-girls in shorts. Chinese-Australian artist Guo Jian has ironically reprised the ballet in numerous paintings that sex up some of its most iconic scenes. But the AsiaTOPA production was a strictly nostalgic affair – technically updated, but politically retro, bereft of subtext.

Many Chinese Australians whose families suffered during the Cultural Revolution or Land Reform found the staging of *The Red Detachment* at one of Australia's premier arts venues offensive and re-traumatising. They protested outside the Arts Centre, alongside some who simply objected to the romanticisation of the Communist Party's violent past.

"Red detachment" is not an option for Australia

Critical reception to the show was mixed. Most reviewers admired the dancers' prodigious skills, though some mistakenly perceived ironic intent. Writing in the *Daily Review*, Maxim Boon described it as a "bizarre mix of elegant, thoroughly Western classical ballet and bombastic military bluster". When the audience "warmly applauded" the production, Boon wrote, it brought to mind the performance of the so-bad-it's-good musical "Springtime for Hitler" in Mel Brooks's *The Producers*.

For what, exactly, do you clap when you applaud such a production: the virtuoso performances; the Cultural Revolution kitsch-trip; the symbolic representation of violence visited upon a group, landowners, to which you may yourself belong? How much easier it is to go see *The Book of Mormon.*

Yet "red detachment" is not an option for Australia today. China under the Communist Party is a rapidly rising and steadily more assertive global power, as well as our foremost trading partner. The PRC's policies and actions affect the strength of Australia's universities, tourism and export sectors; the health of our environment; the security of our food production; the integrity of our political system; and our regional security. The PRC also plays an increasingly important role in the survival of international institutions such as the United Nations, as well as global solutions to climate change.

This country has long struggled with its Asian identity. But Australia is already part of the Chinese world, and the Chinese world is part of Australia. Australia is home to 1.2 million people who claim some form of Chinese ancestry. Many are immigrants or children of immigrants, from Hong Kong, Singapore and Taiwan, as well as from the mainland. Mandarin is today the second-most common language spoken in Australian homes after English.

As for the two global powers that have helped to shape Australia's cultural identity and been our dominant non-Indigenous cultural influences, republicanism will dispatch the antiques roadshow of the United Kingdom from our shores sooner or later. The United States, especially under Trump, is looking like a less reliable and savoury ally every day. The 2018 Lowy Institute Poll found that almost the same proportion of Australians trusted the United States to "act responsibly in the world" (55 per cent) as they did China (52 per cent). More had "some" or "a lot" of confidence in Chinese president Xi Jinping to "do the right thing" (43 per cent) than in Trump (30 per cent).

That's not to say we won't still enjoy and relate to Shakespeare and *Doctor Who*, Hollywood and David Byrne. Whatever happens in geopolitics, we will continue to benefit from linguistic, historical and cultural affinities with the Anglosphere, as well as the European, South American, African and other Asian cultures that enrich our world. But Australia's ability to connect with China on a cultural level is crucial to our ability to understand and deal with the challenges of what is often a frictional relationship.

Chinese culture is many things. It is Peking opera and Beijing punk. It is ancient classics and internet slang. It can be historical, retro, contemporary, highbrow, popular, propagandist or rebellious, and may originate on the mainland, or in Taiwan, Hong Kong or the Chinese diaspora. It is a window into the intellectual and political preoccupations, hopes, dreams, social realities and fault lines within the nation to which our future is so inextricably tied.

The reverse of the West

Words such as "mysterious", "exotic" and "inscrutable" have for centuries attached themselves to China, paradoxically enhancing its romantic appeal while inhibiting appreciation of its more mundane realities. "Oh, East is East, and West is West, and never the twain shall meet," wrote Rudyard Kipling in his 1889 "The Ballad of East and West". Although the poem goes on to defy these assumptions, that first line, liberated from its context, resonates for a reason – especially regarding China. It's possible to understand this in a non-racialised way: the character-based, tonal Chinese languages that underpin China's rich literary, philosophical and artistic heritage present a genuine barrier, keeping "East" and "West" on either side of a linguistic divide. Translation helps Australians see across the divide, but Chinese literacy is a bridge to the other side. Yet while successive Australian governments have championed the cause of Asia literacy generally and Chinese-language studies in particular, they seemingly forget to turn their words to action. One statistic does not speak for a nation, but it is worth noting that in New South Wales in 2018, out of 76,323 students doing one or more HSC courses, only 224 (less than 0.3%) were studying Chinese as a second language.

The official rhetoric of the PRC makes even contemporary China seem weirdly exotic in its insistence that all Chinese think as one: "we Chinese people believe" this; "the Chinese dream" is that; yet another thing "offends the feelings of the Chinese people". Communist Party language around "the People" and "the masses" imposes a fantastical vision of unity on the heterogeneous reality of 1.4 billion people. This is reinforced through spectacular displays of almost hallucinatory indivisibility, such as the 2008 musicians drumming in perfect unison at the opening ceremony of the 2008 Beijing Olympics.

Yet non-Chinese Australians have no reason to think those of Chinese heritage either exotic or unknowable. Indigenous people traded with Chinese fisherman along the northern coast for centuries before the arrival of anyone who even remotely resembled Pauline Hanson. The first, modest wave of Chinese migrants arrived in 1848 as indentured labourers, mainly irrigators and shepherds. More came during the gold rush several years later. Despite anti-Chinese riots and a permeant racism that crystallised in the White Australia policy and still lingers in the far-right corners of our body politic, for over 170

Encounters with China ... have energised the work of many contemporary Australian artists

years Chinese people have been essential to the fabric of Australian society. Some were mainstays of our cultural, social and political life even at the height of White Australia: for example, the businessman, philanthropist and political progressive Mei Quong Tart, whose Sydney tea rooms were the meeting place of Sydney's first suffragettes. Today, numerous individuals of Chinese heritage play a role in mainstream Australian culture: former news anchor Lee Lin Chin, photographer William Yang, children's author and illustrator Shaun Tan, chef Kylie Kwong, senator Penny Wong and writer Benjamin Law, to name just a few. Yet the first Chinese-Australian sitcom,

The Family Law, appeared only in 2016, showing that Australia still struggles with the Chinese part of its multicultural identity.

It's certainly true that, beginning in the nineteenth century, imperialist ideology, theories of race, and missionary writings combined to create in the minds of many white Australians a vision of China as a place of pestilence, cruelty, violence and godlessness. The author of *My Brother Jack*, George Johnston, who was born in 1912, reminisced in a memoir:

> When I was a child in Melbourne, I was terrified of Chinese. They were evil, sinister figures slinking down dark alleys in Hollywood films with long knives concealed beneath their baggy sleeves ... On the few occasions when I had to go down Little Bourke Street ... I would run with thumping heart and terror in my eyes.

("African gangs", anyone?)

In the Cold War period, an abhorrence of communism conjoined with ambient fears and stereotypes so that China, in the broad Australian imagination, became a source of potential ideological infection. A Liberal Party pamphlet from that era even featured a map of Australia over which a plague of red dots was spreading, along with the tagline "STOP THE RED RASH!"

Lachlan Strahan's superb *Australia's China* describes the evolution of Australian prejudices and impressions of China from early contact through to the 1990s. These impressions were far from universally negative. Yet, as Strahan writes, they were all based, to one extent or another, on an idea of China as "the reverse of the West".

In the 1940s, George Johnston went to China as a war correspondent. He later wrote a novel set there, *The Far Road*. Its protagonists are two male foreign correspondents, one American and one Australian. In many English-language novels and not a few memoirs, China essentially serves as the background or proving ground for white men's (and occasionally white women's) dramas and fantasies, both heroic and erotic – a genre mercilessly parodied in George MacDonald Fraser's 1985 *Flashman and the Dragon*.

The Scottish-Australian artist Ian Fairweather represented a different model of artistic engagement with our largest Asian neighbour. Fairweather first went to China in 1929, where he studied the Chinese language and calligraphy; he lived there again for a time in the 1930s. Long after he left, he continued to produce drawings and paintings influenced by Chinese landscapes and the aesthetic traditions of China. Critics today consider him one of the greatest Australian painters of all time.

Encounters with China and its culture have energised the work of many contemporary Australian artists, directors, musicians and writers, from Oodgeroo Noonuccal, who began writing poetry for the first time in years following a trip to China in the mid-1980s, to contemporary visual artist Tim Johnson, whose work draws on Chinese imagery as well as that of other cultures. Today, there are numerous opportunities for Australian artists and writers to visit and work in

China. The Department of Foreign Affairs and Trade, the Australia Council for the Arts, Screen Australia and Asialink sponsor tours, residencies and exchanges, as do several smaller or private entities, from Beijing's Red Gate Gallery, founded by Australian Brian Wallace in 1991, to Australian chef and restaurateur Michelle Garnaut's Shanghai restaurant M on the Bund. The Australian embassy in Beijing, meanwhile, has run an Australian Writers Week since 2007, inviting authors such as Richard Flanagan, Alice Pung, Les Murray and Alexis Wright to talk about their work in several cities across China.

The novelist James Bradley went to Shanghai on an Asialink residency in 2005. He told me in an email that "it was a fascinating experience, and led to a better appreciation of the complexities of China and Chinese society, and an ongoing fascination with its culture". It also made him "intensely aware of just how difficult it is to understand China or Chinese society without good Chinese language skills ... So while I'm deeply interested in China and more aware of its complexities as a result of my time there, I'm also keenly aware just how limited my understanding is."

Before 1972, only about 1000 Australians had ever visited the PRC. Today, more than 700,000 Australians visit China every year. All return with some degree of cultural insight. Australians who may never get to mainland China have more opportunities than ever to encounter aspects of Chinese culture at home: *The Red Detachment of Women*, certainly, but also the exhibitions of twenty-first-century Chinese art at Sydney's privately funded White Rabbit

Gallery, and the work of writers including Yan Lianke, Yu Hua and Liao Yiwu, all of whom have been published in translation by Australian publishing houses Text and Giramondo, to name a few of the most obvious examples.

Still, while most Australians can easily rattle off the names of a dozen or more contemporary American or European musicians, actors, artists, films, television shows or books, I'm guessing that they would be hard-pressed to name even a couple from China. One would almost surely be the cringe-making yet insanely mesmerising dating game show *If You Are the One*, a fixture on SBS since 2013.

We are both more connected than we think ... and less than we probably need to be

Most Australians would have been oblivious to the passing, in October 2018, of a giant of popular Chinese literature, Jin Yong, a mainland-born, Hong Kong–based writer whose cultural footprint in the Sinosphere is analogous, *The New Yorker* has suggested, to that of *Harry Potter* plus *Star Wars*. How many Australians can conjure up the names of China's two winners of the Nobel Prize for Literature, Gao Xingjian and Mo Yan? Yet it was an Australian, Mabel Lee, who translated Gao's signature work, *Soul Mountain*, which was published here months before he was awarded the prize. I reviewed it for *The Age*. When the Nobel was announced, several newspapers around the world quoted from that review, not because it was the best one they could find, but because it was the only one. We in Australia are both more connected than we think we are and less than we probably need to be.

A brief history of infatuation and disillusionment

Voltaire never travelled to China. But the eighteenth-century French philosopher was so taken with Confucianism that he described it as "the purest morality", and China as a model of secular, humane civilisation. In the 1950s, after the American Beat poet Gary Snyder translated the work of the legendary ninth-century hermit poet Hanshan (*Cold Mountain*), the counterculture embraced Hanshan as the embodiment of free-spirited anti-authoritarianism – the ultimate "dharma bum", as Jack Kerouac had it. Beginning in the 1950s and 1960s, radical leftists in Australia, as elsewhere, idealised Mao's China, where, in the credulous testimony of journalist Wilfred Burchett in 1951, "a new life designed to eliminate every tiniest injustice is being built".

Sinophilia is always at least as much about the Sinophile as it is about China. Voltaire was searching for alternatives to repressive Catholic dogma and French governmental institutions. The Beats were rebelling against the socially and politically repressive America of the McCarthy era. Burchett and other "fellow travellers" bristled at the similarly narrow, conservative politics of the Menzies era. The Sinophile, a person who "loves China", is usually in search of, to borrow Lachlan Strahan's phrase, "the reverse of the West". (Sinophile, incidentally, is not an analogue for Sinologist, someone who *studies* China.)

In 1978, the young Australian writer, curator and artist Sally Gray travelled to China on a three-week "women's study tour". In 1999, Gray revisited the experience with an exhibition at Sydney's Casula Powerhouse titled "China '78: A Political Romance". The China of her political imagination, she wrote in the catalogue, "provided a visionary site for thinking about the possibility of social perfectibility and was a model of how socialism, communism, Maoism could bring justice and equality to workers, women and oppressed people of all kinds". Once there, however, she writes, "the 'real China' of totalitarian control kept coming to our reluctant attention". Not long after, she began what she describes as "the long process of de-programming the dream".

Like Gray and her fellow leftists, Cold War ideologues and anti-communists also had to readjust their views on China in the late 1970s. Soon after Deng Xiaoping took control of the Chinese Communist Party in 1978, he began reforming China's top-down "command" economy and opening the country to the outside world. Soon, it would be the conservatives' time to become infatuated, convinced that the introduction of market mechanisms in China would lead to democracy and the end of the Communist Party itself.

That same year, 1978, the Department of Foreign Affairs established the Australia-China Council (ACC), "in the hope", as its inaugural chair, the historian Geoffrey Blainey, has written, "of bridging or lessening the wide gaps, especially in culture, the media, the arts, sport, science and education". When the ACC toured nine figures from the ancient emperor Qin Shi Huang's Terracotta Army in Australia in 1983, nearly one million people around the country queued to view the exhibition. In *The Australia-China Council: The First Forty Years*, editor and China scholar Paul Farrelly quotes an unnamed "local critic" who found the more than two-millennia-old figures "rather crudely executed". Farrelly comments:

> While the *Entombed Warriors* was one of the ACC's early successes, it also encapsulated the challenges faced by the Council: an eagerness for Australian society to engage with China and a hesitance by certain elites to recognise, or even try to understand China's importance.

Other "elites" were faster off the mark. As artistic director of Melbourne's Playbox Theatre, Carrillo Gantner initiated theatre exchanges between Australia and the PRC beginning in the late 1970s. Gantner (who was also, more recently, patron of AsiaTOPA) served as cultural counsellor at the Australian embassy in Beijing from 1985 to 1987. He was succeeded by novelist Nicholas Jose. These appointments, the strong cultural orientation of the ACC and a widespread positivity in Australia about Deng's China, however naively optimistic some of it appears in retrospect, helped make the 1980s a period of energetic cultural exchange and engagement. Film-festival audiences here gave rapturous welcome to China's young Fifth Generation filmmakers, and art schools clamoured to host emerging Chinese artists.

Then came 1989, the student-led, pro-democracy protests and occupation of Tiananmen Square, and the subsequent massacre of unarmed civilians on Beijing's streets by the People's Liberation Army. The news had a visceral impact here; it was the 9/11 of its time. China suddenly seemed less like the great hope and more like the great pariah. Nicholas Jose later wrote that Australia "was hurt by the break-up of its love affair with China. When the outrage wears off, the pain is soothed by confessing that you don't really know what happened, that you never under-stood and that you don't care if you never see her again."

In the early 1990s, Deng ramped up the pace of economic reform, and opened China wider to foreign investment, while relaxing some social controls, including over artistic production and exchange.

The pendulum swing of infatuation and disillusionment ... narrowed to a vibration

Australians hadn't forgotten 1989; culturally, our interest tilted towards more dissident narratives. These included Jung Chang's 1991 memoir *Wild Swans*. Although Chang lived in the United Kingdom, her publishers decided to launch the book in Australia because, as Chang's late agent Toby Eady explained to *The Telegraph*: "They have a curiosity in Australia. They are concerned about seeing things that are happening now ... Australians are interested in other cultures." The book, which was banned in China, became a phenomenal success here, selling around 350,000 copies, and went on to sell more than ten million copies in thirty languages worldwide.

In 1993, Sydney's Museum of Contemporary Art (MCA) produced a landmark exhibition of new Chinese art with an ironic political edge. "Mao Goes Pop" smashed attendance records at the museum. In her book *The Tao: Conversations on Chinese Art in Australia*, Chinese Australian artist Tianli Zu quotes Nicholas Jose saying that one could see the exhibition's impact on high-school students for years afterwards in the work presented in ARTEXPRESS (an annual showcase of outstanding student art). It took until 1998 before an exhibition of similar scale and reach, "Inside Out", was produced in the United States. More recently, the National Gallery of Victoria's 2016 exhibition *Andy Warhol / Ai Weiwei* attracted nearly 400,000 visitors, breaking attendance records there as well; Ai Weiwei, of course, is the ultimate dissident-artist.

Yet as the years passed, Australia's engagement with China, cultural and otherwise, "normalised": the pendulum swing of infatuation and disillusionment, Sinophilia and its obverse, Sinophobia, narrowed to a vibration.

There were still bilateral tensions and the occasional row, some serious, some less so. Pauline Hanson's maiden speech in parliament in 1996, in which she railed against Asian immigration, revived the spectre of White Australia, but its widespread denunciation and ridiculing demonstrated that by the mid 1990s, Sinophobia had all but disappeared into those noisome far-right corners – corners that twenty years later seem suddenly to have expanded into entire rooms.

We need to talk about Clive

Napoleon called China a "sleeping giant". He said, "Let him sleep, for when he wakes ... " The rest of the quotation, about what China will do to the world once awakened, is contested. According to the great translator of French literature, Australian Julie Rose, there are two versions. One uses the verb *trembler*, which, she explained to me, signifies "to quake or shake in fear ... so cautionary (watch out!) ... but also just a bit celebratory (wow!)". The other uses the verb *étonner* – "to amaze, astonish, surprise – so celebratory, or neutral, with no negative connotations". In the four decades since Deng Xiaoping launched his economic reforms, the giant has truly awoken. We quake, shake and tremble; are amazed, astonished and surprised.

In 2008, the spectacle of bussed-in mainland Chinese students threatening pro-Tibetan protesters at the Olympic torch relay in Canberra sparked widespread unease and anger, heightened by credible reports that the Chinese embassy had provided the students with material support. The following year, mainland Chinese hackers took down the website of the Melbourne International Film Festival after it was announced that the festival would screen the documentary *The 10 Conditions of Love*, about the life of exiled Uyghur rights activist Rebiya Kadeer, who was also to be a guest. Beijing ordered the Australian government to "immediately correct its wrongdoings" by cancelling both the screening and Kadeer's visa. Canberra didn't flinch, the website went back up, Kadeer arrived and Chinese protests drew so much attention to the film that the screening had to be moved to a bigger venue, where it sold out all 1500 seats. (Governments never seem to learn that banning something only makes it irresistible.) And so thousands of festival-goers and millions of other Australians who followed the news became, even if by proxy, culturally engaged with yet another dissident narrative from the PRC. If those same people today are energised to petition or protest Beijing's mass internment of Uyghurs in Xinjiang, Beijing can consider it an own goal.

In 2010, Frank Moorhouse withdrew from Australian Writers Week in protest at the harsh sentencing of the cultural critic and pro-democracy activist Liu Xiaobo to eleven years imprisonment for "subverting state authority" just months earlier. Later that year, Liu was awarded the Nobel Peace Prize; his death in custody in 2017 further darkened Australian views of human rights in the PRC. This was exacerbated by the authorities' gratuitous cruelty towards his widow, Liu Xia, under house arrest from 2010. When the dissident artist Badiucao, a naturalised Australian citizen who remains anonymous to protect himself and his family from death threats, painted a tribute to the couple in Melbourne's Hosier Lane, it turned into a shrine.

Quaking and shaking reached fever pitch in Australia with *Power and Influence*, the 2017 ABC/Fairfax investigation into "the hard edge of China's soft power", and the publication early the following year of Clive Hamilton's *Silent Invasion*. Both delivered strong and sensational messages about interference in Australian internal affairs by the PRC and its agents. *Silent Invasion* debuted in second place on the Australian nonfiction bestseller list; its publisher told me that it sold almost 20,000 copies (excluding ebooks) within six months of publication. Hamilton speaks, among other things, of PRC operatives "controlling the Chinese community in Australia", and claims to have "robust" evidence that the Chinese Communist Party is "engaged in a systematic campaign to infiltrate, influence and control the most important institutions in Australia" and turn Australia into a "tribute state". It's hard to judge how much influence such views have, but the 2018 Lowy poll quoted earlier found that 82 per cent of Australians surveyed perceived China to be "more of an economic partner" than "a military threat".

A simplistic reading of Chinese culture leads to simplistic conclusions

Hamilton disparages people who believe in continued engagement with China as the "China lobby", "apologists", "Panda huggers", "dupes", "innocents" and even "appeasers", evoking both the Cold War and the Third Reich while tapping into deeper historical anxieties. He quotes a diplomatic defector who insists that Australia's "openness" and multiculturalism, as well as its large Chinese immigrant community, leave us especially vulnerable to Beijing's manipulations.

But Hamilton, who does not speak or read Chinese, doesn't get everything right about China. As an example of how the CCP promotes a "common ethnic consciousness" of Chinese identity to shore up its legitimacy and extend its "global reach", Hamilton writes: "The hugely popular song 'Descendants of the Dragon', a karaoke favourite approved by the party, exalts those with 'black hair, black eyes, yellow skin'."

My book *The Monkey and the Dragon* tells the strange and complicated history of that song (which I translate as "Heirs of the Dragon") and its composer, Hou Dejian, whose grandmother's torture is mentioned earlier in this article. Hou, the son of mainlanders who followed Chiang Kai-shek to Taiwan in 1949, was a student and folk singer there in 1978, when the United States announced that it was breaking relations with Taipei to establish them with Beijing. Observing his classmates' grief and fear, he wrote "Heirs of the Dragon" as a mournful meditation on Chinese identity. He never imagined that the song, born of specific circumstances in Taiwan, would become a virtual anthem across the Sinosphere in the 1980s, including in the mainland. (If he had known, he wouldn't have sold the copyright for around US$150.) In 1989, it was a favourite of pro-democracy protesters in Tiananmen Square. Hou was living in Beijing then. In the square, he met Wu'erkaixi, one of the student leaders. Wu'erkaixi, a Uyghur, did not have "black hair, black eyes, yellow skin". Realising how unintentionally narrow and racialised those lyrics were, Hou changed them on the spot, leading the students in a singalong with the new lyrics. Hou joined a hunger strike, spoke out against the government in the months after the massacre and was forcibly returned to Taiwan a year later, after which the Party banned both him and the song for many years.

Yes, today, people tend to sing it the old way, and the PRC has embraced it. But for others, it still evokes the spirit of 1989. When the Sydney Theatre Company put on the play *Chimerica* in 2017, which centres on the events and aftermath of the Tiananmen protests, director Kip Williams chose this complex song, full of yearning and sadness as well as pride, for the play's musical theme. What Hamilton saw as uninflected ethnic Chinese propaganda, Williams recognised as a cultural artefact of history, meaning and depth.

A simplistic reading of Chinese culture leads to simplistic conclusions about China. Sometimes we quake when we might be astonished.

A tale of two videos

Papi Jiang is a Chinese internet celebrity and comedian. At the height of her popularity, her videos on Yuku (China's equivalent of YouTube) had 44 million followers. Her first live broadcast, in 2016, attracted more than 74 million views in one day, which, as *The New York Times* noted, was more than Taylor Swift's "New Romantics" received on YouTube in four months. Papi Jiang's delivery is rapid-fire, deadpan and, before the censors ordered her to sanitise her language in 2016, was peppered with swear words. Both her comic sensibility and the subjects of her satire – Chinese drunks, the annoying habits of new lovers, Shanghainese Chinglish – betray a contemporary, urban sensibility that is the reverse of the "reverse of the West". Subtitles cannot keep pace with the speed of her monologues or capture the genius of her language-based humour.

So unfortunately, they're inaccessible to non-Chinese speakers.

Equally unfortunately, what is overly accessible are videos churned out by the Party's many clueless soft-power creatives, like 2018's "I'd Like to Build the World a Road", marking the fifth anniversary of the Belt and Road Initiative. It begins with the portentous clicking of a woman's heels on a hard floor. The woman is young, solemn and dressed in a floaty white gown embodying some vague notion of ancient China. To the tune of the 1971 song spawned from a Coke ad, "I'd Like to Teach the World to Sing", she intones: "I'd like to build the world a road, and furnish it with love …" Soon she is joined by other young people, Chinese and non-Chinese, who, with varying degrees of gormlessness, ability and enthusiasm, sing along to this plagiaristic paean to China's international aid-and-development project: "It's the Belt and Road, what the world wants today …"

In his 2017 article in *Foreign Policy*, "Why is China So … Uncool?", the Chinese-American scholar George Gao describes the "quest for cool" as the "key" to soft power. He recounts another one of what he calls China's "most cringe-worthy efforts", the hip-hop video "This Is China", produced by China's Communist Youth League and the rap group Chengdu Revolution. Among the English-language song's deathless lyrics: "First things first, we all know that China is a developing country. It has large population [sic] and it is really hard to manage." And: "As for scientific achievement, we have [Nobel prize winner] Tu Youyou, who discovered artemisinin."

"China's golden age was so admirable," Gao writes, "that, even today, China's propaganda department peddles its ancient cultural products abroad – in part because it has nothing else, really, to offer. The fact that a country invented gunpowder brings it only so much social capital." He quotes the cheeky mainland celebrity blogger, writer, filmmaker and racing-car driver Han Han: "That's like if your girlfriend's family asks if you are wealthy, and you tell them that your ancestors are wealthy," he noted. "It is useless."

Party propaganda does not always play well in China, either. In a (mis)calculated appeal to younger viewers, the makers of the 2017 film *The Founding of an Army* cast Chinese teen idols as historical revolutionary Party leaders. The social commentator Hong Huang, who grew up around actual revolutionary Party leaders (her stepfather was China's foreign minister under Mao, from 1974 to 1976), described the result as "hilarious", not least because young audiences had fun projecting "modern-day romantic narratives on the founding fathers". The previous year, the big-budget propaganda film *My War*, a historical drama about the Korean War, was promoted with a trailer in which a group of elderly tourists cheerfully tell their South Korean guide that they'd been to her country before, "carrying the Red Flag". Chinese social media erupted at the trailer's insensitivity to the suffering of South Koreans during the war.

> **Under Xi, control and censorship ... grows stricter by the day**

These are among many examples that complicate the simplistic vision of witless patriotism and "brainwashed" masses promoted by the new Cold Warriors. Take the runaway success of the aggressively nationalistic *Wolf Warrior 2*, which came with the tagline "Whoever offends China will be killed no matter how far away they are" and broke all Chinese box-office records. Yes, a good part of the film's appeal is its vision of a strong China that rescues its citizens in crisis situations abroad, while punishing its enemies. But *Wolf Warrior 2* was also widely considered the first Chinese film to achieve genuine "Hollywood-standard" action sequences – why wouldn't mainland Chinese audiences go for a film of the sort America produces by the dozen, but in which a muscular *Chinese* hero saves the day? As with Hou Dejian's "Heirs of the Dragon", there's always more to the story.

Mainland Chinese students and others in Australia who have felt marginalised or victimised by the racist fallout from the debate over Beijing's influence took succour from *Wolf Warrior 2*'s vision of a powerful China that protects its own. When I interviewed Badiucao for *China Story Yearbook 2017*, which I co-edit for the Centre for China in the World (CIW) at the Australian National University, he told me he wishes that Australians would engage more with Chinese students and recent immigrants. He noted that social isolation makes them vulnerable to manipulation and influence by the Party and its agents here. These last include Chinese-language media that promote what Geremie Barmé, founding director of CIW, calls a "surround-sound

Chinese cultural-intellectual world ... at loggerheads with Australia's aspirational multicultural society".

On chinaheritage.net, Barmé publishes many of the voices in China and the Chinese diaspora who do not conform to that "surround-sound" world. You can find them in other English-language forums as well; you just have to look. The China Media Project quotes Luo Jianbo, head of the China Foreign Policy Center at the Central Party School in Beijing, as excoriating the "explosion of narrow-minded nationalism and exclusionism that has followed recent frustrations and difficulties in our foreign relations". He called for "confidence without arrogance, pride without conceit". Even the Chinese Communist Party is not homogeneous.

The Party is, however, run now and into the conceivable future by Xi Jinping, an unabashed authoritarian who would dearly like to impose ideological conformity of the sort the new Cold Warriors believe already exists in China. Under Xi, control and censorship of the arts and media grows stricter by the day.

Chinese artists, writers and musicians continue to create as best they can. Some play *cabianqiu*, "edgeball" – a strategy in table tennis where one hits the ball on the edge of the table in such a way that it's impossible to return, but still legal. The indie band Carsick Cars have a cultish international following, including in Australia, where they have toured; the lyrics of one of their most famous and enigmatic songs repeat, over and over, "Zhongnanhai", the name of the Party's leadership compound just west of the Forbidden City.

Engagement is not surrender

Among the offerings at the recent 2019 Sydney Festival was the premiere of an Australian children's play in which a twelve-year-old girl goes to China to scatter her mother's ashes. Another was a collaboration by Australian and Chinese dancers and musicians. There was a retrospective by the controversial Chinese-Australian artist Xiao Lu, and *Shànghǎi MiMi*, "a sumptuous cabaret" inspired by 1930s Shanghai and starring an international cast of singers, dancers and acrobats from China, Cameroon, Australia and France.

Genuine engagement isn't always as simple as attending (or creating) a festival show. As with *The Red Detachment of Women*, participation can at times raise sticky questions. And while cultural engagement in general may enrich us intellectually and socially, it is not going to solve Australia's economic or political problems with the PRC, some of which are confounding and serious. But it does make it less likely that we will resort to the kind of racism and facile name-calling and stereotyping that can only sabotage our ability to interact and negotiate with the country that looks set to dominate geopolitics in our region for some time to come. Besides, to equate cultural engagement with political surrender implicitly endorses the idea that Chinese culture is the preserve of the Communist Party – what's more, it denies the Chinese people themselves complexity, agency and creativity. ■

THE ROOKIE PMS

How Canberra's leadership
circus is damaging ties with Asia

George Megalogenis

"We do not claim to be Asian." This provocative statement defined
John Howard's first overseas trip as prime minister in September
1996. He meant no offence to his host, Indonesian president Suharto,
and none was taken. In fact, the comment generated little discussion
at the time because it was self-evidently true. Australia's ethnic face
was Anglo-European. Barely 5 per cent of our population was born
in Asia, and the projections at the time had the figure creeping up to
7.5 per cent by 2025.

"Are we reverting to England?" would have been the more appro-
priate question at the dawn of the Howard era, because immigrants
were still coming from the mother country while the waves from Italy,
Greece and Yugoslavia had long dried up. In 1996, the English-born
in Australia outnumbered immigrants from southern and eastern
Europe and from Asia.

"I do not believe that Australia faces a choice between our history and our geography," Howard told the Indonesians and the travelling Australian press corp. "Neither do I see Australia as a bridge between Asia and the West, as is sometimes suggested."

The reference to the "bridge" did cause a stir because it seemed to undermine the purpose of the address, which was to reassure our neighbours that his newly elected government would remain an "active participant in the region". Howard thought the criticism was overblown and was slow to clear to air. "These words were followed by others which put them in proper context, yet for several days the press wrote of a 'blunder'," he explained in his memoir, *Lazarus Rising*.

But Howard underestimated the baggage he was carrying on that first official visit. Six days earlier, Pauline Hanson had used her maiden speech to parliament to call for a return to the White Australia policies of racial selection and industry protection. In a region where one-party rule was the norm, even in democracies such as Japan or Taiwan, it was easy for the misunderstanding to take root that Hanson was speaking for the Australian government, even though she sat on the crossbenches. Hanson's line, "we are in danger of being swamped by Asians", was compared with Howard's apparent distancing of Australia from Asia.

Howard did go to Jakarta with domestic politics in mind, but he wasn't thinking of Hanson. He was still brooding over a campaign sledge from his arch rival, Paul Keating. As the 1996 election barrelled towards the inevitability of a landslide Coalition victory,

Keating had made the extraordinary claim that Asian leaders would not deal with Howard. In Jakarta, Howard no doubt wanted to show Keating, and perhaps prove to himself, that Asia would not only welcome him to the leaders' club but accept him on his own terms, as a proud Australian.

The first impression of a man out of his depth might have stuck if Howard had lost office in 1998, or 2001. But he had time to grow into the job. Slowly, he learned to lift his gaze from the headlines back home and appreciate the perspective of the people in the room. By 2003, he was playing host to US president George W. Bush and Chinese president Hu Jintao on consecutive days. And in 2004, he earned the affection and respect of the new Indonesian president, Susilo Bambang Yudhoyono, with his generous aid response to the Boxing Day tsunami. From uncomfortable novice to elder statesman, it took many years of trial and error on the international stage to find the sweet spot between diplomacy and domestic politics.

> **Howard matured in the role of prime minister [but] none of his successors have held the job long enough**

I was reminded of Howard's uncertain regional debut when Scott Morrison, our fifth prime minister in the past five years, changed the location for misunderstanding from Jakarta to the eastern suburbs of Sydney, where the government was facing a difficult by-election. The seat of Wentworth had been vacated by former prime minister

Malcolm Turnbull after the August 2018 coup against his leadership. Morrison inserted himself into the final stages of the election campaign by suggesting that Australia would move its embassy in Israel from Tel Aviv to Jerusalem. He was presumably pitching to the large Jewish population in the electorate, because there was no apparent logic beyond Wentworth – it is plainly absurd to think that a newly installed Australian prime minister with no prior experience in foreign affairs would suddenly emerge, saviour-like, to bring peace to the Middle East. No country asked Morrison to build a bridge between the Israelis and the Palestinians. Yet there he was, a leader without a domestic mandate playing statesman outside his own region, seemingly without giving a moment's thought to how this policy shift would be received by Indonesia or Malaysia, which supported the Palestinian cause.

The steps to what quickly became a crisis are worth recounting because they point to a wider systemic problem in our body politic. It has become the habit of every prime minister since Howard to view Asia through the wrong end of the telescope, placing domestic concerns above all else and assuming that our neighbours will forgive our insensitivity when we ask them to play along. But while Howard matured in the role of prime minister, none of his successors have held the job long enough to leave a positive legacy. Inevitably, this will tarnish Australia's image in the region, as our temporary prime ministers become known only for their rookie diplomatic errors and the manner of their dismissal.

Morrison had enjoyed a charmed run to national leadership. Whereas Howard slogged for twenty-two years before becoming prime minister at his second election attempt, Morrison fulfilled his ambition in half the time, without having to face the people, and without blood on his hands – a critical break with the habit of Liberal and Labor predecessors, from Billy McMahon to Malcolm Turnbull, and from Bob Hawke to Julia Gillard.

The position fell into his lap after the Home Affairs minister, Peter Dutton, challenged Turnbull for the leadership last August. Dutton had gathered just enough support in the party room to cripple Turnbull, but not a majority to replace him. Morrison, the nation's treasurer for the past three years, was the compromise candidate. His luck appeared to be overflowing because his first act as prime minister was to fly to Jakarta to sign a free trade agreement with Indonesian president Joko Widodo. The deal had been handed to him on a platter by Turnbull, who had been settling the fine print just before the coup.

All went according to plan on the day. Morrison recited the mantra that every Australian prime minister since Keating takes to Jakarta. "The partnership between Australia and Indonesia is one of our nation's most significant," he announced. "Indonesia is playing, and will continue to play, a much greater role on the global stage, particularly in the areas of economy and security." As a senior member of the government, Morrison might be expected to understand what those words meant.

Australia's overriding interest is for Indonesia, the world's largest majority Muslim nation, to remain an ally in the fight against regional terrorism, and to become an active partner in setting the governing norms for the Asian Century to ensure all countries are treated fairly and China's unilateral impulses are checked. Australia has a direct interest in Indonesia's success. It needs Indonesia to join China, Japan and India in the top ten economies of the world, both for its own continued prosperity and to maintain balance in the region. The key to this engagement is openness and mutual respect.

Morrison displayed neither in his handling of the Jerusalem question. He placed the issue on the table with a Trumpian disregard for process, and in the white heat of a by-election campaign. Morrison did not consult those in foreign affairs and defence, who would likely have advised caution, and little effort was made to prepare the Indonesians or the Malaysians for such a radical shift in policy. Morrison overturned decades of pragmatic neutrality on the Middle East in a single bout of poll-driven panic. Just six weeks separated his trip to Jakarta and the kite-flying on the Israeli embassy. Tellingly, the world learned of his interest in Jerusalem on the same day that Palestinian foreign minister Riyad al-Maliki was visiting Jakarta. The fallout was as predictable as it was swift. Indonesia placed the ratification of the free trade agreement on hold until Morrison clarified his policy, while Malaysia's prime minister, Mahathir Mohamad, warned that relocating the embassy would add "to the cause of terrorism".

Morrison scrambled to save face. He asked Turnbull to meet with Jokowi to explain his position. The move was reminiscent of the mop-up operations that Tim Fischer and Alexander Downer, respectively the deputy prime minister and the foreign affairs minister in the Howard government, would undertake in the 1990s to assure the region that Pauline Hanson did not speak for Australia. Later, Morrison announced a final policy position that pleased no one, recognising West Jerusalem as Israel's capital but stepping back from an embassy move to Jerusalem.

This was a rookie error on an epic scale. For Morrison, there was no domestic return for the international risk. The government lost the by-election anyway, and with it, its parliamentary majority. The domestic lesson was the same as the international.

Morrison ... the Australian leader with thin credentials in foreign affairs

Morrison could not see the condescension in his approach, or the offence it might cause at home, let alone abroad. He presumed that Jewish Australians in this electorate placed the symbolism of an embassy in Israel above all else. He bet they would forget that the Liberal Party had executed their popular local member, or that the government didn't take the science of climate change seriously, or that it was still holding children hostage on Nauru in the name of border protection. These were the issues driving Liberal voters in Wentworth to switch to Independent Kerryn Phelps. Cosmopolitan, not tribal, and tolerant, not sectarian, they were just about the last voters in the country who would wish to validate US-style identity politics.

What most troubled about this episode was the careless disregard Morrison showed for the national interest. He violated a basic Australian value – that immigrants not carry the baggage of the Old Country with them. He was pontificating and barracking in the most volatile region in the world without apparent concern for the precedent he was setting. Imagine a future Labor prime minister, facing a by-election in Sydney's west, inserting themselves into the Middle East peace process on behalf of the Palestinians. For a politician blinded by data, it would be an easy mistake to make. There are 604,000 Muslim Australians, according to the 2016 Census (and they outnumber Jewish Australians across the country by six to one). Morrison did not understand the field he was playing on. What sort of Australia would we be living in today if previous leaders, stirred by crude domestic calculations, had picked a side in, say, Northern Ireland's Troubles, or the breakup of the former Yugoslavia? The voters of Wentworth did the nation a favour by rejecting the Morrison ploy. They kept their politics where it belonged, in Australia.

Morrison's ordeal should have ended there, with a valuable lesson learned. But at his debut on the global stage – in Buenos Aires in late November for the annual meeting of the G20 – Morrison, now three months into the job, found that he, and by extension Australia, had become a punchline. US president Donald Trump asked him what had happened to Malcolm Turnbull, while German chancellor Angela Merkel carried a picture of him in her briefing notes and didn't try to hide it. The flippancy from Western powers was, in its way, more wounding than the fury of Indonesia and Malaysia. It signalled that Morrison's ascension, the fourth to occur outside a general election in a decade, was the tipping point to international ridicule. Of course, this wasn't Morrison's responsibility alone. It was just his misfortune to be the leader who had to answer for a decade of dysfunction.

Morrison is the most extreme example yet of the Australian leader with thin credentials in foreign affairs. Howard established the pattern two decades earlier. He was the first Liberal prime minister of the post-Menzies era without any experience in the Foreign Affairs portfolio, or in the domestic portfolios involved in the project to open up Australia to the world. He didn't have Harold Holt's background in Immigration, or John Gorton's or Malcolm Fraser's in Defence, or Billy McMahon's in the old External Affairs ministry. This is not to suggest that prime ministers before Howard were gaffe-free – Gorton and McMahon, enemies in the party room, were fellow travellers in cringeworthy diplomacy. But there was an expectation back then that politicians made an effort to understand Asia (even when we didn't want its people).

The majority of Howard's twenty-two years in parliament before he became prime minister were consumed by a leadership tussle with Andrew Peacock, who, ironically, was the foreign affairs minister when Howard was treasurer in the Fraser government. The next

Liberal prime minister, Tony Abbott, served an apprenticeship of nineteen years that was notable for the things he helped stop – he led the "no" campaign at the republic referendum in 1999, and ten years later he ended the bipartisanship on climate change policy. His successor, Turnbull, had been in parliament for just under eleven years when he became prime minister.

Immaturity also defined the Rudd–Gillard government. While Kevin Rudd had been a diplomat before he entered parliament, neither he nor Julia Gillard had much experience in national government when they took office as prime minister and deputy in 2007, after just eight years in parliament together, and only a year as a leadership duo. Perhaps Rudd would have grown into the job if Gillard had resisted the push to remove him in 2010. Perhaps Gillard might have led a long-term government if Rudd, in turn, hadn't undermined her leadership.

What made this inexperience an even greater handicap for us in the region was the increasing concentration of power in the prime minister's office. Howard may have started with a blind spot on Asia, but he was an old-school politician wedded to orderly Cabinet process. He gave himself every chance to learn on the job because he took advice. By contrast, Rudd and Gillard – and then Abbott – preferred to make captain's calls. That placed their rookie diplomatic errors in another category to Howard's, because they sprang from a relatively new flaw in our system. Morrison didn't consult on Israel because he had no other model for governing. He entered parliament at the 2007 election, which Labor won with a presidential campaign built around one man, "Kevin 07". Rudd's instinct was to govern alone, and his party allowed it while his approval rating was high. It was Rudd's disregard for Cabinet process that saw him test the friendship with Indonesia over asylum seekers. Gillard repeated the error when she suspended the live cattle trade without warning on the strength of a television program. Abbott, learning nothing from his predecessors, got into a public slanging match with Indonesian president Yudhoyono after it was revealed that Australia's intelligence agency had tapped the phones of Yudhoyono and his wife, Ani. Morrison's embassy play followed recent practice by assuming that the prime minister knew best.

Creative diplomacy ... was replaced by the knee-jerk of domestic politics

In each of these cases, backing down was not an option because no Australian leader wants to admit error to a foreign country. A more-experienced operator, working in a more balanced political system, would have delegated authority to the foreign affairs minister and their department, leaving the issue to be resolved quietly, without the crisis accelerants of local media deadlines and opinion polls.

The leadership coups might not have mattered if the government of the day maintained a consistent approach from one prime minister to the next. But each spin of the roulette wheel triggered an abrupt change in policy. The critical issue for Australia now is: will the circus of our politics cause lasting damage to our interests in the region?

Consider how the rivalry between Rudd and Gillard shaped Australia's border protection regime and warped relations with our neighbours. According to Gillard, one of her first major arguments with Rudd followed the *Oceanic Viking* incident in October 2009. This was the Australian vessel that had rescued Sri Lankan asylum seekers on their way to our shores. Rudd wanted the passengers to return to Indonesia, where their claims for protection would be assessed. But they would not leave the vessel until they had been promised resettlement in Australia. One month passed before a deal was finally struck. In its assessment of the standoff, the US embassy in Canberra wrote that Rudd's "megaphone diplomacy" had placed President Yudhoyono in a difficult position. "The Indonesian public don't want to be a dumping ground for what they perceive [to be] Australia's problem," said a cable to Washington dated 18 November 2009.

Gillard was more worried about the local reaction. "Kevin seemed determined to ignore the increasing number of asylum-seekers arriving by boat and the damage the *Oceanic Viking* incident had done to the government's standing," she wrote in her autobiography, *My Story*. Gillard wanted a tougher border protection policy, but Rudd resisted. It was clearly a sore point between them because on the night Gillard challenged for the leadership, in June 2010, Rudd warned his colleagues that he would not be "lurching to the right on the question of asylum-seekers as some have counselled us to do".

Once in the prime minister's office, Gillard got ahead of herself by indicating that asylum seekers would be sent to East Timor for processing. She hadn't consulted the East Timorese government, and the plan was quickly killed off. The next port of call for a solution was Malaysia, but the High Court ruled Gillard's resettlement agreement unconstitutional. She sought to address the court's concerns through special legislation, but the Abbott-led Opposition joined with the Greens to block her path. She withdrew the legislation to avoid losing the vote in the House of Representatives, leaving Australia without an effective border protection regime for the remainder of her minority government. Notice the trend? Each argument between leadership rivals dragged in a neighbour who was expected to relieve Australia's burden. The creative diplomacy that had been a hallmark of our engagement in Asia for a generation was replaced by the knee-jerk of domestic politics.

When Rudd reclaimed the Labor leadership in June 2013, he disowned Gillard's approach and outflanked Abbott with a policy so cruel that it was bound to affect our international reputation. Rudd called on Papua New Guinea to provide a new detention facility on Manus Island. The asylum seekers transported there would never be allowed to settle in Australia. Rudd intended to wind up the measure after the election. But Labor lost in a landslide, and the new prime minister, Abbott, had the political luxury of implementing a policy much harsher than the one he had campaigned on. Abbott added indefinite detention and "turning back the boats" to the regime, thereby completing Australia's transformation to neighbourhood bully.

Three and a half years and another prime minister later, Turnbull explained the brutal logic to Trump.

"Why haven't you let them out? Why have you not let them into your society?" the newly elected US president asked Turnbull in their infamous telephone conversation in January 2017.

"It is not because they are bad people," Turnbull explained. "It is because in order to stop people smugglers, we had to deprive them of the product. So we said 'if you try to come to Australia by boat, even if we think you are the best person in the world, even if you are a Nobel Prize winning genius, we will not let you in'."

"That is a good idea," Trump agreed. "We should do that too. You are worse than I am."

Is this really how we want to be known in the Asian Century – as the spoilt rich country that engages when it suits, and pushes its anxieties onto its neighbours when domestic politics calls? The tragedy is that this aggrieved, entitled posture undermines our greatest strength in the Asian Century: our people.

Last year, as the government imploded, Australian society quietly crossed the threshold to majority immigrant. More than 50 per cent of the population now is either born overseas or has at least one parent who is an immigrant. The last time we were here as a people was in the 1890s. Back then, we were closing the doors. The first draft of the White Australia policy had already been written to ban Chinese immigration to the colonies. Ahead was half a century of stagnation as the combination of immigration restrictions and industry protection undermined our standard of living.

It would take a wilful act of national self-sabotage to recreate the equivalent policy settings in the twenty-first century. No one is suggesting that the tariff wall go back up. Our trade surplus with Asia has averaged more than $70 billion per year in the decade so far. The surplus with our neighbours exceeds the combined deficits with Europe and the United States by $7 billion per year. On the other hand, calls to slash immigration are coming back into vogue. Abbott, Dutton and the New South Wales government and Opposition have led the campaign. To his credit, Morrison has resisted the pressure for a gratuitous cut. His stint as treasurer taught him that immigration has been the main driver of economic growth since the end of the mining boom.

The face our leaders present ... is certainly not who we are

Immigration is at the heart of the Australian paradox in Asia. Our demography is Eurasian but our politics remains much whiter than the nation it serves. Only 6 per cent of the parliament has non-European or Indigenous heritage, compared to 24 per cent of the broader Australian population, according to a report by the Australian Human Rights Commission in 2018.

There are inevitable lags between the arrival of an immigrant wave and their representation in the nation's power structure. Rushed entry of a recently arrived skilled immigrant into parliament might be counterproductive because they could not be expected to know their electorate. But mass immigration from Asia has been a feature of Australian life for forty years now. It's high time the gap was closed.

I can't help but think there is a direct relationship between the increasing volatility of our politics and the narrowness of the gene pool. The late John Button, industry minister in the Hawke and Keating governments, was among the first to warn of the dangers of a parliament dominated by apparatchiks. In his 2002 Quarterly Essay, *Beyond Belief,* Button compared the socially diverse Labor Party that took office in 1983 under Bob Hawke with the blander version that almost reclaimed government in 1998 under Kim Beazley. The first Hawke ministry included "former farmers, businessmen, academics, lawyers and union officials, as well as a former engine driver, a teacher, a retailer, a waterside worker and a shearer," he wrote. "The government that reformed and deregulated the economy was not made up of political mandarins." The class of 1998 was predominantly drawn from Labor's political and industrial wings. "Out of the 96 members, 53 came from jobs in party or union offices. These members described themselves variously as 'administrators,' 'officials' and 'electoral officers.' There were also 10 former members of state parliaments and nine described as political consultants, advisers and lobbyists." That intake included Rudd and Gillard.

The Liberals, who repeated Labor's history of removing leaders between elections, were drawn from a similar political class of advisers and lobbyists. Abbott was the first prime minister on the conservative side to have worked as a political staffer before entering parliament. Gillard was the first for Labor.

Diversity is not just a matter of ethnicity or socioeconomic background. The largest gap between parliament and the people is gender. Women have accounted for the majority of the professional workforce since 2004, yet they were just 32 per cent of members and senators elected in 2016.

The face our leaders present to the world – white, male, impatient and easily offended – is certainly not who we are as Australians. When Howard said "we do not claim to be Asian", he was speaking on behalf of a country that was exhausted by social and economic change.

Howard had wanted to slow the rate of Asian immigration in the late 1980s, but his stance cost him the Opposition leadership. He apologised for those comments as a precondition for his resurrection in 1995. The balance of power within the Liberal Party still resided in Victoria, where support for multiculturalism was non-negotiable.

Howard liked to remind journalists who doubted his conversion that his electorate of Bennelong, in Sydney's inner north-west, had one of the largest Asian populations in the country. Howard had no real argument with Paul Keating's government on economic or social policy. The key issue in the 1996 campaign, the combatants agreed, was who we wanted to be as a nation: Howard's comfortable and relaxed

Australia that owed no apology to anyone versus Keating's independent, reconciled Australia that had atoned for the sins of a racist past. It was identity politics before the term became fashionable, and the fault line it exposed runs through our politics to the present day.

Howard walked both sides of the street, accepting diversity and enabling the backlash against it in older, whiter electorates. It was good for one landslide, only because people were sick of Keating. Once in government, though, Howard found himself in a perpetual argument between the future and the past.

The 1996 election provided an early sketch of what an Australia polarised by ethnicity would look like. Twenty years before Brexit and Trump, our electorate was divided between the parochial and progressive. For the first time in federal history, the Coalition won more seats in Queensland than in Victoria. At the 2010 and 2016 elections, Labor won a majority of seats in New South Wales, Victoria, South Australia and Tasmania. In the past, the party that won the two largest states would have been guaranteed majority government. But the Coalition hung the parliament in 2010 and held a majority of one in 2016 because it enjoyed landslides in Queensland and Western Australia.

When weighing the difference between Queensland and Victoria then and now, one statistic that stands out is immigration. Queensland remains our least Asian state on the mainland, while Victoria is the most Asian. There is another difference. The Coalition party room was 80 per cent male after the last election. Labor was much closer to equality – 56 per cent male and 44 per cent female.

Howard became prime minister at a time of transition. The Asian financial crisis, democracy in Indonesia, East Timorese independence, the *Tampa* affair and the rise of China were all ahead of him. At home, the wheels of demography were turning towards the inevitability of higher immigration from Asia to counter the effects of an ageing population.

It is easily forgotten in the shrillness of the debate between Howard and Keating, but they were arguing against a backdrop of slower immigration rates. The formal end of the White Australia policy coincided with a global economic crisis. Unemployment and inflation were handbrakes on Australia's immigration program, which meant that the first wave of migrants to arrive from South-East Asia, starting in the 1970s, was not as large as the European wave that preceded it.

Are we Asian yet? It's complicated

But 1996 would prove to be the twilight of old Australia. The following year, the Asian-born population overtook the English-born for the first time in our history. By 2007, Howard's final year in office, the Asian-born outnumbered the European-born.

The past two decades are comparable to the postwar wave, but with a twist. Today the Asian-born population is approaching three million, or around 12 per cent of total residents, almost double the proportion that was expected when Howard took office. The combined

English and European total is 2.4 million (10 per cent). But this group is much older than the country at large.

The twist is that the majority of those who have arrived since 1996 did so under the skilled-migration program. The previous waves from England, Europe and South-East Asia began their Australian journey on the lower rungs of the income ladder, and were distributed more evenly across the country. The skilled immigrant lands between the middle and the top, and most settle in our two largest cities. Between them, Sydney and Melbourne include 40 per cent of the national population, but have 75 per cent of the Chinese-born, 74 per cent of the Sri Lankan–born, 73 per cent of the Vietnamese-born and 64 per cent of the Indian- and South Korean–born in Australia. Of the seven main groups from Asia, only those from the Philippines and Malaysia have substantial communities outside our twin Eurasian capitals. But they still have more than half their populations in Sydney and Melbourne.

Are we Asian yet? It's complicated. The answer is yes in the booming inner city and outer suburbs of Melbourne, Sydney and even parts of Brisbane. Already the Asian-born outnumber the Australian-born in Melbourne's inner city, and in Auburn, in Sydney's west. They match the Australian-born in Melbourne's Dandenong, Sydney's Parramatta and Brisbane's Sunnybank. But the rest of the country is either still in transition or caught in a time warp, with an ageing Anglo-European population that is not being replenished with new immigrants.

Australia will struggle to reconcile this complexity while the major political parties continue to appeal to their tribes, with the Coalition relying on white male voters, and Labor on cosmopolitan females. Targeting these groups does not win over the nation at elections; ultimately, it leaves the parliament gridlocked and undermines faith in democracy. Trust in government has been in freefall since the first leadership coup, in 2010. At the last election it was at an all-time low, and the major parties achieved their lowest combined primary vote since the 1930s.

To break the cycle, Labor and the Coalition need to build new electoral bases that unite young and old Australia. They can only do this by opening their doors to candidates that better reflect who we are: more Asian, more diverse in gender and experience. A truly representative democracy would relieve the parties of the burden of identity politics by forcing them to appeal to voters as Australians with common interests, rather than as members of rival tribes. This rule-by-inclusion should refocus domestic politics on concerns that matter and allow us to engage more confidently in the region, comfortable and relaxed in our Eurasian skin. The alternative is another decade of minority governments, strained foreign relations and reputational decline, as our neighbours embrace the Asian Century despite us. ■

CAN AUSTRALIA BE ONE OF US?

The view from Asia

Sarah Teo

In October 2010, the eighth Asia–Europe Meeting (ASEM) Summit in Brussels was a significant moment in the longstanding debate over Australia's place in Asia. When it was formed in 1996, this cross-continental grouping required a clear delineation of Asian and European countries. The latter were relatively straightforward to pinpoint: members of the European Union. Identifying Asian countries was more complicated. The then seven member states of the Association of Southeast Asian Nations (ASEAN), along with China, Japan and South Korea, were, naturally, considered Asian. But framing Australia and New Zealand as Asian was more contentious. Their attempts to join ASEM when it was first established failed following Malaysia's opposition over doubts about their Asian identity. In 2010, however, Australia and New Zealand were formally admitted.

Identity is a tricky thing. It is fluid, often contested and notoriously difficult to pin down. In this part of the world, the notion of

regional identity is particularly challenging because competing clas-
sifications – "Asia", "East Asia", "Asia-Pacific", "Indo-Pacific" – offer
different interpretations. But perception is important in international
affairs: it drives states' behaviour. Whether Australia is viewed as
Asian or non-Asian by its neighbours affects, in part, how Asian countries approach it and their responses to its foreign policy initiatives.

When examining regional groupings, Australia's status as an
Asian country depends on which nation is asked, and about which
issues: demographics, security, economics, contributions to aid,
regional memberships. So it is most revealing to consider Australia's
immediate neighbours and the few countries that are vocal on its place
in the region. These include Indonesia, Malaysia, the Philippines and
Singapore. China and India are also important, due to their size and
the population of these diasporas in Australia.

From this starting point, one overall trend dominates the narrative of Australia's regional image. While Australia's place in the region
is often ambiguous, it is still generally perceived as an outsider to Asia,
with stronger cultural and political ties to the Western world.

Anglosphere affinities

Australia has come a long way since the White Australia policy.
Multiculturalism enjoys bipartisan support, and over the last two
decades the proportion of the country's population born overseas
has risen steadily. From 2007 to 2017, the percentages of those born
in England, Italy and Scotland declined, but the proportions of those

born in China, India, the Philippines, Vietnam and Malaysia increased. The number of Australian residents with Chinese ancestry rose from about 3.4 per cent in 2006 to 5.2 per cent – or 1.2 million people – in 2016, while the number of those with Indian ancestry increased from 1.2 per cent to 2.6 per cent – or 620,000 people. Student enrolments from Asia have also risen over the past decade. As of October 2018, students from China made up the largest share of Australia's international students, at 30 per cent, followed by India (13 per cent), Nepal (6 per cent) and Malaysia (4 per cent). In quantitative terms, Australia is more "Asian" than it was a decade ago.

These numbers demonstrate Australia's desirability as a place to live. The country has had

Australia ... continues to be perceived as an outsider

twenty-seven years of uninterrupted economic growth, has one of the highest minimum-wage levels in the world, and its people enjoy a relatively strong level of political freedom. Australia has consistently ranked within the top three of the United Nations Development Programme's Human Development Index, which is based on life expectancy, education levels and standards of living. Its universities are considered among the best in the world. A 2016 survey conducted by the Institute of Policy Studies in Singapore found that Australia was the preferred migration destination for local respondents, far ahead of New Zealand, in second place, followed by the United States, the United Kingdom, Canada and Japan. Travelling from Asia to Australia has become easier and, in most cases, cheaper. Ten years ago, direct flights connected Australia and mainland China only between Sydney and Melbourne, and Beijing and Shanghai. Today, there are more than 100 flights a week between multiple Australian and Chinese cities. In 2016, Singapore Airlines became the first carrier in more than a decade to fly regularly to Canberra from overseas. With expanding transport and people-to-people links, Australia appears to be becoming increasingly "Asian-ised".

Yet most of Australia's population remains of Anglo-Saxon ethnicity. Although the proportion of first-generation immigrants born in England has declined, it is, at 4.1 per cent, far higher than that of any other foreign country. Despite the rapid increase in the number of Australians with Chinese ancestry, the 2016 ABS census found that the most common groups of ancestry continue to be English (33.6 per cent), Australian (31.2 per cent), Irish (10.2 per cent) and Scottish (8.6 per cent). While ethnic compositions differ across cities and suburbs – and there are parts of Sydney and Melbourne where those with Chinese or Indian ancestry are the largest population group – the Asian presence in Australia, though expanding, still forms a relatively minor segment of the overall population.

While views of Australia's Asian-ness have evolved since the late 1980s, as its links across the region deepened, it continues to be perceived as an outsider. It is safe to say that many in Asia see Australia's closest cultural affinity as with its Anglosphere partners, such as the

United States and the United Kingdom. In the 1990s, Asian statesmen such as Singapore's Lee Kuan Yew and Malaysia's Mahathir Mohamad attributed Asia's economic rise to social cohesion and order, as well as to a belief that collective goals supersede individual gain. These values were framed in contrast to Western ideals, which promote liberal democracy and individual rights. While the debate over "Asian values" may have faded following the 1997 Asian financial crisis, the differences in the cultural underpinnings of Australia and Asian countries persist. Australia prides itself on its liberal values and democratic system of government. English is the dominant language, with more than 70 per cent of the population speaking it at home. The percentage of Mandarin and Vietnamese speakers may be on the rise, but according to the 2016 census they comprise only 2.5 per cent and 1.2 per cent of the population respectively. Queen Elizabeth II remains the nation's head of state.

Of course, Asia is neither monolithic nor a static entity. There is no single common language across Asia. Different Asian countries have different levels of regard for liberal values and democracy – for example, while Indonesia and the Philippines have introduced freedom-of-information laws similar to those in Australia, others, such as Singapore, have so far been more cautious. Moreover, demographics in Asian countries are changing, with many cities becoming more cosmopolitan – a development that is intensifying as societies become more technologically advanced and virtual barriers are broken down. Perhaps the question is not so much whether Australia could be considered an Asian country but whether Australia and Asian countries are, over the longer term, moving towards some sort of cultural convergence as both evolve and as the lifestyles of their populations become more similar.

Casting off the deputy sheriff badge

Another way to examine Australia's Asian identity is to look at the country's approach to regional security and economics. Australia's prominent role in the Timor-Leste crisis in the late 1990s has often been held up as an example of its diplomatic insensitivity towards Asian countries. Indonesian leaders and officials accused Australia of interfering in the country's domestic affairs – a diplomatic taboo in the Asian context. The accompanying "Howard Doctrine", which then Australian prime minister John Howard unveiled in an interview with *The Bulletin*, also met with an unwelcome reception from South-East Asian countries. Howard expressed his belief that Australia was seen to have unique responsibilities in the region thanks to its "special characteristics" as a "European, Western civilisation with strong links with North America" but geographically located in Asia. He added that Australia's leadership of the multinational peacekeeping force into Timor-Leste had "cement[ed] Australia's place in the region", and that the country could afford to be a "participant on our own terms" in Asia. Howard further fanned the flames by agreeing with a journalist who framed Australia as a regional "deputy" to the United States' global sheriff. This was roundly criticised by South-East

Asian policymakers, who retorted that Asians could take care of their own region. Following 9/11, the Howard government once again found itself in hot water when the prime minister said that he would consider pre-emptive strikes on Asian countries to prevent terror attacks in Australia – a statement several South-East Asian nations interpreted as a threat to their sovereignty.

In the last decade, relations between Australia and South-East Asian countries appear to have moved past those diplomatic controversies. Asian countries have turned to Australia for assistance with crises and disasters. Malaysia has been one of the more vocal critics of Australia's approach towards Asian nations, yet in 2014 it called on Australia,

Australia remains closely wedded to its "great and powerful friends"

along with Indonesia, to lead the search efforts for missing Malaysian Airlines flight MH370 in the southern Indian Ocean. Expressing gratitude, then prime minister Najib Razak described Australia as an "invaluable friend". Australia has also contributed to humanitarian assistance and disaster relief missions around the region, including after Cyclone Nargis in Myanmar in 2008, the Sumatra earthquakes in Indonesia in 2009 and Typhoon Haiyan in the Philippines in 2013. In the wake of Haiyan, Philippines president Benigno S. Aquino III commended Australia for working "towards building a truly inclusive, resilient and stable region". Australia's efforts have gained it a great deal of goodwill from its neighbours, and helped to shape perceptions of it as an important stakeholder with much to offer in the most disaster-prone region in the world.

Australia's contributions extend to development assistance for neighbouring countries. While Australia's overseas development assistance budget has fallen since the mid-2010s, South-East Asia and East Asia remain the second-largest recipient region, and Indonesia, Timor-Leste, the Philippines, Vietnam and Cambodia are among the top ten recipient countries. In several South-East Asian countries, Australia is among the ten largest donors and offers valuable help for developing economies.

Investment figures, though, paint a different picture. As a source of foreign direct investment, Australia falls outside the top ten in most Asian countries. Meanwhile, the lion's share of its overseas investment continues to go to the United States (29.1 per cent in 2017) and the United Kingdom (14.6 per cent), with Japan following at a distant third (5.5 per cent). The other Asian countries in the top ten are mainland China (3.4 per cent), Singapore (2.6 per cent) and Hong Kong (2.1 per cent). While statistics alone may not reflect the complexity of Australia's place in Asia, these figures reveal the extent to which Australia remains closely wedded to its "great and powerful friends".

Similarly, key elements of Australia's approach to security continue to be anchored in its Western – rather than Asian – ties. Australia is not just a US ally; it is the only country in the world to have fought alongside the superpower in every major conflict over the past century. It is part of the Five Eyes network, an exclusive intelligence-sharing platform among five English-speaking countries: Australia, Canada, New Zealand, the United Kingdom and the United States. At the United Nations, Australia is considered a member of the Western European and Others Group, rather than the Asia-Pacific Group. This has implications for elections to UN positions that are based on geographical representation. These characteristics set it apart from other US allies in the region such as Japan and South Korea – and this shapes Asian perceptions of Australia.

Australia's close ties with the United States were illustrated in December 2018, when Prime Minister Scott Morrison announced that Australia would recognise West Jerusalem as Israel's capital. This followed the Trump administration's similar recognition in 2017 and the subsequent relocation of its embassy. Morrison's earlier proposal – made before the Wentworth by-election in October 2018, reportedly to attract votes from the Jewish community – had also raised the possibility of Australia shifting its embassy to Jerusalem, to the chagrin of Muslim-majority countries in the region. Indonesian foreign minister Retno Wulan described the potential move as a "slap [to] Indonesia's face on the Palestine issue". While Morrison appears to have backed away from the relocation, Australia's recognition of West Jerusalem as Israel's capital remains a thorny topic with some in the region. Malaysia's foreign ministry issued a statement "strongly oppos[ing]" Canberra's decision, with Mahathir warning that Australia's policy change would "stir more anger" over the subject. Australia has the unquestionable sovereign right to make its own foreign policy decisions. But it would be useful to remember that its neighbours may interpret these decisions in ways that do not match Canberra's intentions.

This episode reflects Australia's perennial challenge as an Anglosphere country located geographically close to Asian countries that do not necessarily share its values, beliefs and outlook on global developments. Compared to the contentious assertions and bitter recriminations between Australia and South-East Asian countries during the Howard era, Australia's contributions to regional security and economics in the past decade have improved relations and enhanced appreciation of its role in Asia. Yet the image of Australia as a strong US ally and a Western country endures; after all, this is Australia's reality. Intentionally or not, much of Canberra's foreign policy – on issues such as the war in Afghanistan or Chinese investment in sensitive assets – aligns with Washington's, perhaps more so than the foreign policies of Tokyo or Seoul. Consequently, Australia will continue to be seen as distinct even from those in the region who are US allies.

More "Pacific" than "Asian"

Within the international community, Australia's status as an Asian country could be justified by its founding membership in several of Asia's key multilateral platforms. Perhaps most significant was its leadership in the creation of the Asia-Pacific Economic Cooperation (APEC). As Cold War tensions wound down in the late 1980s, Australia seized the initiative to convene APEC, and the first ministerial meeting was held in Canberra in November 1989. This met with strong opposition from the first Mahathir administration, which proposed an alternative East Asia Economic Group (EAEG). These two groupings reflected competing visions of the region: Asia-Pacific and East Asia. Mahathir argued that because the EAEG was meant to represent the Asian voice when negotiating with Europe and the United States, countries such as Australia and New Zealand – which "always favoured the European viewpoint" – should be excluded.

The phrase "rules-based order" has become loaded with an anti-China connotation

While the EAEG foundered in the early 1990s due to a lack of regional support, APEC grew in significance, with a leaders' summit added in 1993 at the suggestion of then prime minister Paul Keating. Australia's success with APEC arguably offered some validation of its regional identity.

Australia has also been part of the ASEAN Regional Forum (established in 1994), the East Asia Summit (2005) and the ASEAN Defence Ministers' Meeting-Plus (2010) since their inaugural meetings – although its role in these platforms was not as crucial as in APEC's formation. Australia's membership of these institutions reflects its Asian neighbours' recognition that it belongs to the same broad region that ranges geographically from India in the west to the United States in the east. In March 2018, then prime minister Malcolm Turnbull hosted an inaugural ASEAN–Australia Special Summit in Sydney, marking a high point in Australia's relations with the South-East Asian forum.

Yet the view of Australia as an outsider in Asian regional architecture persists to an extent. Countries such as Malaysia and China were initially disinclined to include Australia in the East Asia Summit. At the first meeting in 2005, which included Australia, Malaysian prime minister Abdullah Badawi stated: "I don't know how the Australians could regard themselves as East Asians." Granted, Australia's actions leading up to the summit did not aid international perceptions. When talk surfaced in late 2004 of an impending East Asia Summit, Canberra appeared dismissive. The Howard government was initially reluctant to sign ASEAN's Treaty of Amity and Cooperation in Southeast Asia – a criterion of East Asia Summit membership – arguing that the treaty's terms clashed with Australia's US alliance and would obstruct Australia from speaking out against, for instance, human rights abuses in member countries. While Canberra later acceded to the treaty on condition that it would not restrict Australia's foreign policy and security relations, this episode reinforced differences over regional identity and values with "East Asian" countries – and it also reinforced certain pre-existing perceptions of Australia's dedication to its Western allies.

The fate of Kevin Rudd's "Asia-Pacific community" proposal is another example. During a speech in June 2008, then prime minister Rudd proposed the formation of an Asia-Pacific community by 2020, taking inspiration from the European integration process. Implicit in the concept was that a core group of countries – Australia, China, India, Indonesia, Japan, Russia, South Korea and the United States – would occupy a more central role than others in the region. The response from regional officials, including former Australian prime ministers, was characterised by caution and criticism, particularly because Rudd had not consulted with neighbours before announcing the initiative – a process highly valued by ASEAN and East Asian countries alike. The Asia-Pacific community did not eventuate, although Rudd has drawn parallels between his proposal and the expanded East Asia Summit that materialised in 2011. It has been a decade since the proposal, but as Tang Siew Mun, the head of the ASEAN Studies Centre at ISEAS-Yusof Ishak Institute in Singapore, observed in 2018, memories of Rudd's proposal, a "concept which all but bypassed ASEAN", are still fresh "in the region's strategic consciousness".

Given this context, the most recent multilateral initiatives involving Australia – the Quadrilateral Security Dialogue (the Quad) and the Indo-Pacific Strategy – have drawn suspicion from some in the region. According to a survey of South-East Asian perceptions of the Quad, conducted by Huong Le Thu from the Australian Strategic Policy Institute, the US-backed network of like-minded maritime democracies including Australia, Japan and India has prompted some concerns about how it would engage with a rising China and how it fits with the existing ASEAN-centred regional security architecture. Australia is also seen as part of a group of US allies supporting Washington's Free and Open Indo-Pacific strategy, which highlights the importance of democracy, freedom of navigation and rules in global affairs – elements linked to countering Chinese influence in the region. Moreover, Canberra has positioned itself as an ardent defender of the rules-based order. Support for the role of international institutions and norms would no doubt be welcomed by Australia's medium-sized and small neighbours, but the phrase "rules-based order" has become loaded with an anti-China connotation that not many regional countries want to be associated with.

These different visions of regional cooperation reflect individual countries' commitments to ASEAN, their relations with China and the United States, and the values and priorities that guide their foreign policies. These variations not only distinguish Australia from Asian countries, but are evident across Asian countries themselves. For instance, the outlook from Vietnam – which has endured domination by and war with bordering Chinese dynasties for centuries – is unlikely to resemble Indonesia's. Even South Korea and Japan, technically next-door neighbours and both US allies, have displayed different attitudes towards increasing Chinese influence, with Tokyo much more enthusiastic about the Indo-Pacific strategy.

Countries in the region, Australia included, share a pragmatism that guides their respective policies towards a rising China and its potential displacement of US leadership in the regional order. Despite being a US ally, Australia has not given in to US calls for Australia to conduct freedom-of-navigation exercises within 12 nautical miles of disputed islands in the South China Sea. Australia's response to China, like that of any other country in the region, is carefully calibrated by its national interests and overall foreign relations.

This illustrates the complexity of defining regional identity and belonging. How Australia is perceived as a member of the Asian region is an aggregate picture of its status as a US ally, its commitment to and promotion of liberal democratic principles, its affiliation to the Anglosphere, and its approach towards regional groups and development. In regional groupings, Australia is generally perceived as belonging to the "Pacific" – as reflected in the concepts of the "Indo-Pacific" and the "Asia-Pacific" – rather than definitively "Asian".

Australia could position itself as a constructive and supportive member of the region

How to make the most of an ambiguous identity

Even though Australia is now more entrenched in Asia – through its demographics and regional engagement – than several decades ago, it was still described by Mahathir as recently as March 2018 as an "outpost of Europe". Perception is based on character plus circumstance. The perception of Australia's regional identity stems from its status as a US ally, its history and population, and its willingness to take part in "Asian" community-building efforts.

Australia may be a valuable member of the region – however broadly this is defined – but culturally it would be hard to make the case that it is currently seen as an Asian country. Perhaps we should accept that Australia's identity and place in the region are characterised by ambiguity and ambivalence – both in the way it views itself and how it is viewed by others – and likewise so is the concept of Asia.

There are productive ways in which Australia could deal with its complex and occasionally ambiguous status. It is crucial to be aware of the cultural sensitivities that arise from dealing with Asian countries, and to display this awareness in interactions with leaders and diplomats. Australia should be well-positioned to do this, due to its changing population and growing links with its Asian neighbours.

Also, Australia can play to its strengths. It will continue to be viewed as a close friend of the United States and of the "Western" world in general, and these ties afford it some advantage, given that many Asian countries view the US presence in the region as essential for stability and economic prosperity. Ideally, Canberra should use its links to Washington to enhance its standing as a valuable member of regional groupings. However, it also must be careful not to overplay this hand and become perceived as working to curtail China's rise or being dismissive of the smaller states in the region; neither would help it to build a positive image or achieve closer relations with its Asian neighbours.

Australia's strength also lies in the fact that it is a developed economy and technologically advanced. By utilising these assets, Australia could position itself as a constructive and supportive member of the region – for instance, in providing humanitarian assistance and helping to build up Asian countries' capacity to deal with natural disasters.

There is no doubt that Australia's links to Asia will expand in the years to come, both in terms of demographics and politics. Ultimately, its future status and identity in the region will depend on how it interprets its place in Asia, and how it reflects this interpretation through its policies – and whether this alters perceptions among its Asian neighbours. ■

THE FIX

Solving Australia's foreign affairs challenges

—

Sam Roggeveen on the Case for a Larger Indonesian Diaspora

"There is no more important foreign relationship for Australia than that with Indonesia. Canberra should draw on migration policy to send a message of solidarity and trust."

THE PROBLEM: Calls for Australia to launch a nationwide effort to dramatically deepen our ties with Indonesia are a regular feature of our foreign policy debates. But these appeals often come without specifics, or the measures proposed are either unattainably ambitious or too modest to deliver more than incremental change.

Why do we need a "step-change"? Our political leaders tend to focus on opportunity. If Australia doesn't pay attention to Indonesia's burgeoning middle class, our politicians argue, we will miss our chance to profit. Australia's biggest worry, in this telling, is a bad case of economic FOMO.

Yet the real reason to focus on Indonesia is not opportunity but risk. Australia and Indonesia have suffered numerous diplomatic breaches and security disputes. Indonesia now stands on the cusp of great-power status – it has the potential to become, over the first half of this century, a nation whose strategic clout in Asia is surpassed only by China and India. For Australia, the costs of any potential rift with Indonesia are increasing.

The dilemma is sharpened by a rising China. Canberra does not want Beijing to dominate South-East Asia. To prevent this, Australia has no alternative but to work with Indonesia, because nothing Australia can do alone is likely to be enough. Even if it strengthened its defence capabilities dramatically, the effort would be pointless were Indonesia to slide into China's orbit.

Ultimately, Canberra should aim to forge a military alliance with Jakarta. But because that goal remains so distant, the best we can do for now is to encourage closer defence cooperation.

Economically, there may also be limited scope for improvement. The two economies have little complementarity, and even a free trade agreement won't fix major obstacles in Indonesia such as corruption, price controls and a weak legal system.

More aid is also not the answer. As defence strategist Hugh White has written, "No one likes receiving charity because giving is, among other things, an expression of power – especially between states." Indonesia is a nascent great power that Australia cannot treat as a mere client.

So how can Australia add ballast to the relationship with Indonesia to avoid sinking it over minor controversies (beef, boats and boogie boards) and to ensure it can meet the needs of the Asian Century?

THE PROPOSAL: Australia should play to its strengths, and one thing it has proven exceptional at – the best in the world, perhaps – is migration. Former prime minister Malcolm Turnbull's claim that Australia is the most successful multicultural nation on earth was no idle boast.

Australia should aim to substantially increase the number of Indonesian permanent residents. A larger diaspora would build ties between Indonesians at home and those in Australia; as commentator George Megalogenis has written, "every migrant is a potential emissary". This would also make Australians more familiar with Indonesia, as a culture and as a country, and could have positive economic side effects for Indonesia.

Most importantly, such an initiative would signal that Australia sees its future as inextricably linked with Indonesia's and wants the two nations to grow together. Australia is tied irrevocably to the fate of South-East Asia, so this would demonstrate a long-term commitment to its relationship with the region's biggest power.

Indonesia has played a relatively small part in Australia's migration story, particularly compared to less strategically important South-East Asian nations. The Department of Home Affairs ranks Indonesia nineteenth as a source country for Australia, behind the Philippines (fifth), Vietnam (sixth) and Malaysia (ninth). In 2014, 81,140 Indonesian-born people were living in Australia. To sharpen Australia's message about Indonesia's importance, that number should rise dramatically.

WHY IT WILL WORK: Australia's migration debate tends to focus on domestic issues such as environmental capacity, strains on infrastructure and services, and impacts on housing and employment. When Australia's place in Asia is invoked, it is often in terms of whether Australia needs more migrants to build a larger defence force.

But to see the true importance of Australia's migration model to its place in Asia, we should consider the alternative – what if Australia stopped all migration or drastically cut the intake?

Economic growth would slow and the gradual Asianisation of the population would be suspended. Canberra would soon be dealing with Jakarta from a position of weakness. While Indonesia continued its growth, Australia would have chosen to arrest its integration with Asia while its economy and defence capabilities went into relative decline. Australia would be an outsider, a declining asset, and increasingly vulnerable to coercion as the power balance in Asia shifts. Yet if Australia opts for continued growth with an increasingly Asian face, it presents to Jakarta as a partner with valuable military capabilities and diplomatic assets, a nation with no racial hang-ups, and one that is better to have as a friend than as an adversary.

There is Australia's alliance with the United States to consider, too. A growing Indonesia will become more important to the United States. Canberra cannot risk a crisis with Jakarta in which Washington is forced to choose sides, because the Australia–US alliance is no guarantee that the United States would choose Canberra. And if, as some predict, the United States were to withdraw from the region, the problem would become even more acute. The 2016 Defence White Paper forecasts that Indonesian defence spending will match Australia's by 2035; in those circumstances, a breach with Jakarta could be very costly.

There would be a price for building a larger Indonesian diaspora. One reason for Indonesia's low migration levels to Australia is that too few Indonesians meet Australia's stringent skills requirements. Australia could not simply target Indonesia's most qualified, because Jakarta is sensitive to the issue of "brain drain", so Australia would need a separate intake of Indonesian migrants who may be less economically productive and may make higher demands on government services. But Australia doesn't only need university-educated migrants; it needs others, too. For instance, tens of thousands of Indonesian care-givers already work overseas, and given rising demand in Australia's aged-care sector, this could be an attractive starting point.

It is not unprecedented for Australia to target its migration program for foreign-policy purposes. The Pacific Labour Scheme is an example, as is the Abbott government's decision to take in 12,000 Syrian refugees, and Bob Hawke's offer of asylum to Chinese students after the Tiananmen Square massacre. In their own way, each was a statement of foreign-policy priorities – Australia used its migration program to signal to its citizens and to the world its values, responsibilities, interests and aspirations.

In the twenty-first century, there is no more important foreign relationship for Australia than that with Indonesia. Canberra should once again draw on its greatest policy strength to send a message of solidarity and trust.

THE GOVERNMENT'S RESPONSE: The Department of Home Affairs said it was committed to continuing to "deepen" the relationship with Indonesia but did not say whether it supported or opposed allowing a specific intake of Indonesian migrants. A spokesperson said Australia's skilled migrant program was non-discriminatory and noted that Indonesia was a signatory to Australia's working holiday program, which allows short-term working visits for people from both countries. ∎

Reviews

Identity: Contemporary Identity Politics and the Struggle for Recognition
Francis Fukuyama
Profile Books

Caution defines both the arguments and the style of Francis Fukuyama's *Identity*. It is not difficult to surmise why this might be so. Fukuyama, who has a distinguished CV as a political economist and an academic, is most famous for his 1992 book *The End of History and the Last Man*, an expansion of a 1989 essay. That essay and the subsequent book developed an argument, influenced by Hegelian philosophical precepts, that the end of the Cold War had made possible an end to political and cultural struggle, with "the universalization of Western liberal democracy as the final form of human government". The triumphalism of which Fukuyama was accused is not entirely fair. The essay title, after all, was posed as a question. Yet a rereading of the book is instructive. The blindness to non-European philosophical and political history now seems staggeringly myopic.

I remember at the time that for many people on the left, all of us dealing with the knock-out punch delivered by the collapse of communism, Fukuyama was often derisively labelled a "neoconservative". That was a largely thoughtless response to an argument that was far more nuanced and anxious about liberalism than the pronouncements and writings of more ideologically driven neoliberal economists and political actors. Fukuyama was not Milton Friedman, and he was certainly no Dick Cheney. But the hubristic folly that led to the West's involvement in the catastrophic wars in the Middle East also undergirded much of *The End of History and the Last Man*. The two planes that flew into the Twin Towers in New York City in 2001, and the subsequent tragedy of the destruction of Iraq, seemed to deliberately mock his theory. And in a different sense, but in similarly spectacular fashion, so did the emerging of communist China as a global economic superpower.

So, yes, Fukuyama's new book is deliberately cautious. The focus again is on the importance of the European Enlightenment in developing universal notions of equality and justice and freedom. Though he has written previously about the danger of utopian thinking to political society, he is a covert idealist. What he doesn't adequately address is how liberalism as we now know it has no "pure" essence but is forged from the ongoing conflict and compromises between labour and capital, and from the complicated history of nations throwing off the yoke of colonialism. Again, there is scant attention paid to nations and history outside the European and Anglophone world, and I started annotating my copy of the book with questions. Why do some nations develop a social-democratic form of liberalism? Why for others is it

more laissez-faire, and for others still a conservative and statist form of democracy? Trying to corral the myriad forms of liberalism into an epochal cosmopolitan and globalised unity, Fukuyama overlooks one of liberalism's great strengths: its resilient and pragmatic promiscuity.

The main philosophical advance he attempts in *Identity* is to introduce a concept borrowed from Plato – *thymos* – to buttress his arguments. Though he has written of this ancient Greek notion before, in this book he makes it central to his analysis. Fukuyama identifies *thymos* as "the part of the soul that craves recognition of dignity". In its positive guise, *isothymia* is the demand that one be recognised as the equal of one's fellow citizen. In *megalothymia*, the overriding impulse is the desire to be considered superior to others. For Fukuyama, this constant tension between the democratic and authoritarian aspects of *thymos* – which could also be loosely translated as "will" – explains much of the contemporary distrust of liberal democracy, as well as the global turn towards populism.

I think his speculations on *thymos* are seductive and interesting, but here again I am wary of the idealism that overdetermines his analysis. He notes the devastating effects of the Great Recession, and he raises inequality as a key issue that modern democracies must address. But he doesn't explore the relationship between *thymos* and economic injustice: why the claims for dignity only became a political problem with the advent of the global financial crisis. He remains a classic liberal, committed to the notion that only liberalism can provide both economic wealth and long-term social justice, and that means he is on surer ground when examining the struggles of women and people of colour through the lens of *isothymia*. He stumbles, however, whenever addressing class. He is never clear, for example, as to when class demands for dignity are just or when they are populist expressions of authoritarian *megalothymia*. It is understandable that he wishes to defend globalisation and free trade for enabling so much of the world to have emerged from poverty and destitution in the last half century. He is absolutely right to do so. But to put it bluntly, whatever the tensions in nationhood, gender, race and migration that have been

simmering under the body politic for much of the democratic world over the last quarter century, it was an *economic* crisis that brought them to a head. Fukuyama introduces the concept of *thymos* and then refuses to integrate it into an economic analysis of contemporary liberalism. It is a great failing in the book.

I think he also elides something else that is essential to *thymos*: that there is always an aspect of fury – a visceral, disruptive indignation – in the demand of that particular assertion of dignity. For Plato, in *The Republic* and in *Phaedrus*, *thymos* was a third component of the human soul, alongside our logic or reasoning and that of our appetites, and it was logic that could control the dangerously eruptive potentials of *thymos*. The assertion of dignity in the ancient world invariably had a martial component, and the connection between *thymos* and the warrior caste is even explicit in Plato. Fukuyama nods to this connection but then does nothing with it. He is deeply committed to the rational liberal subject, and so the question of whether rationality should guide our actions, emotions and appetites is moot: of course, the answer is in the affirmative. But in ignoring the tensions between logic and *thymos*, he loses an opportunity to explore the key factors that unite the contemporary identity politics of both the left and the right: self-righteous rage and wilful irrationality.

In the second half of the book, Fukuyama directly addresses the turmoil in liberal identity politics that on one hand has led to Brexit, the Trump presidency, nationalism and the authoritarian turn in European politics, and on the other to the idiocies of separatism and infantilism that now bedevil progressive politics across the Western world. The usefulness of *thymos* as a category of investigation for political economy is stretched in these sections, particularly as he is reluctant to incorporate psychology into his analysis, to allow for unconscious or repressed factors that affect our will and our behaviour. He identifies the importance of the Great Recession in fuelling the anxieties of white and European identitarians, but fails to grapple with the ferocity of moral and existential outrage that energises them. The tentativeness of his approach is a real

weakness here. He wants this long essay to be analytical rather than polemical, to avoid the anger and hectoring – and the partisanship – that so dominate the writing around identity at this moment. But it isn't disrespectful to the legacies of the civil rights movement in the United States, for example, or to second-wave feminism or to early gay liberation to try to make sense of the vanity and narcissism that is so central to contemporary hashtag and university-campus politics. Fukuyama notes how working-class politics have been increasingly captured by right-wing populism across the West, but he isn't prepared to indict the bourgeois self-regard that dominates academic, media and student identity politics. There's something more than the desire for dignity going on in this constant avowal of trauma and injury as the defining component of activism.

As a result, one reads *Identity* without ever finding illumination or surprise. The book doesn't have the urgency and charge of some other recent books on identity, also from the United States. Mark Lilla's *The Once and Future Liberal: After Identity Politics*, for example, written directly after the 2016 US election, is caustic in criticising contemporary progressive politics for abandoning the working class. Jonathan Haidt and Greg Lukianoff's *The Coddling of the American Mind* is also a livelier and more engaging examination of the sociological factors that have led to contemporary identity activists trading freedom for safety. In comparison, Fukuyama's book seems stolid. He doesn't investigate what is clearly one of the most confusing and distressing aspects of contemporary politics: how all identity politics is justified in terms of *isothymia*, the wish for equal regard, but in their proclamations and demands what the identitarians all seek is *megalothymia*, the desire that the world remake itself in their image.

It is only in the last chapter, "What is to be done?", that some fire animates his writing. He stresses the need for liberal politics to "create identities that are broader and more integrative" and that "one does not have to deny the potentialities and lived experiences of individuals to recognise that they can also share values and aspirations with much broader circles of citizens". His suggestions are pragmatic and

thoughtful. He defends the notion of the nation-state, and argues cogently that liberals and social democrats shouldn't abandon the nation to extremists and xenophobes. I think he is acute in criticising left-wing and progressive actors for dealing inadequately with fears and anxieties around migration. He is also persuasive in his argument that forms of national service might be one way to build more cohesive citizenship in democracies. It is a failing of both social democracies and liberal democracies that their proponents have deliberately ignored the alienation, family breakdown and hopelessness – and the under-employment and inequality – that so many young people have experienced in the turmoils of rapidly globalised capitalism. It strikes this reader that, alongside a fully funded and adequately resourced public education sector, forms of mandated civil service are indeed a means to ameliorate this tragic historic oversight.

I finished reading Fukuyama's book just as the *gilets jaunes* protests erupted in France. What seemed striking was the incomprehension of the rioters' demands expressed both in traditional media and on social media. Whatever one's analysis of what happened on the streets of France, a demand for dignity – for being seen – was part of what led to the protest. That's the fury that has emboldened #metoo and #blacklivesmatter. It is the same anger, the *thymos*, that has ignited the rise of nationalism and #whitepride. The questions that were being asked, over and over, were whether the French protestors were left-wing or right-wing: which side were they on?

The symbolic resonance, with 2018 being the fiftieth anniversary of Mai'68, is just too delicious to ignore. In 1968, the student replaced the worker as the subject of history. For a generation or more, left-wing theorists have privileged the university over the workplace, and in doing so their thinking has become increasingly obtuse and disconnected from the lived experiences of the majority. I'm not suggesting a turning back of the clocks, a reinstating of the "noble worker". But if one of the challenges of liberalism is to argue its case against the identity politics that is seeing people turn increasingly to the simplistic and xenophobic solutions of the far right, an equally important challenge is for it to refute the narrowness and narcissism of a left-wing politics dominated by the concerns and priorities of the student. I don't want to live in the monocultural and racist world of the right-wing identitarian, but I certainly don't think that means I have to settle for the victim-obsessed politics that now defines the left: who the fuck wants to live in a twenty-four-hour crèche?

I respect Fukuyama stripping anger and rage from his arguments, but his timidity is self-defeating. He clearly believes that liberalism is central to continuing equality, freedom and justice in the world. He and his fellow liberals should be defending it more rigorously.

Christos Tsiolkas

Dreamers: How Young Indians Are Changing the World

Snigdha Poonam
Hurst Publishers

Some years ago, I worked as a teacher and mentor to young Indians who had been admitted into the inaugural Young India Fellowship program, a group of men and women handpicked from across the country who had elected to take on an untested liberal-arts fellowship rather than more traditional postgraduate options. They were a disparate bunch: an environmentalist from rural Orissa, a lawyer from New Delhi, a South Indian engineer, even the daughter of a rickshaw puller. What bound them together was their intelligence and their drive: all wanted to make something of themselves in this new, confident India that was so different from that of their parents' generation.

My job was to help finesse their writing and speaking skills. Each had ambition and focus in spades, and I thoroughly enjoyed spending time with them, inhaling their enthusiasm and quick wit. My one-on-one sessions were sometimes illuminating in other ways, such as witnessing how quickly the rural daughter shed her demure country skin and acquired the shiny-haired hauteur of Delhi girls. Or when an aspiring lawyer from a gem-trading family tried to bribe me to write an essay in his name for the annual Ayn Rand Foundation Institute's student essay contest. "There's a prize of up to $2000," he implored, turning his palms skyward. "I get the title, but you keep the money."

To him, the transaction was perfectly, entirely rational. He spent our hour-long session debating my refusal, in a way that made me think he was using it as an opportunity to hone his courtroom skills. "Here in India, this is how we do things. We all want things to get ahead. Some of us want money" – here, he pointed at me – "and some of us want prestige and recognition. This is just an essay, yes, but why can't we approach it the way we approach a business deal? You get something, I get something. We all benefit."

I was reminded of this encounter while reading Snigdha Poonam's *Dreamers*. The Delhi newspaper journalist spent years trawling cities and small towns, the internet and social media to get a glimpse of how India's youth is faring. What she found was a group of people pursuing different paths but bound by common themes: ambition, nationalism and anger.

"This is a generation of Indians hanging between extremes," writes Poonam. "They are hitting adulthood with the cultural values of their grandparents – socially conservative, sexually timid, god-fearing – but the life goals of American teenagers: money and fame. They have the bleakest chance at a real opportunity – one million Indians enter the job market every month; perhaps 0.01 percent find steady jobs – but the fanciest possible ideas about success."

The core of *Dreamers* is this gulf between the ambitions of Indian youth and the stark reality of the job market.

India right now is in the grip of a demographic opportunity/crisis. The median age is twenty-five, and 600 million Indians – half the country's population – are younger than that. Six hundred million: just let that figure sink in. It is almost twice the population of the United States, almost ten times the population of the United Kingdom, and *twenty-four times* the population of Australia. No other country in the world has a greater number of young people. A youth bulge like this can be advantageous for an economy if handled correctly. However, without the necessary investment in job creation, it can also mean millions of unemployed youth, idle and disaffected – and increasingly angry. It looks like this latter scenario could take hold in India. The Modi government is working hard to create jobs, but to address this situation, it faces the seemingly insurmountable task of creating one million new jobs a month.

Significant investment is also needed in education. According to 2012 statistics, India needs to create 1000 universities and 50,000 colleges by 2022 to meet the demand for tertiary education. Even then, graduates are hardly job-ready, with less than half considered to be employable straight out of university. (Because of this, many organisations provide on-the-job training to graduates, and pass the costs on to their new employees, forcing them to sign illegal bonds that require them to pay back a high percentage of their wages if they leave the company within a year or two – something my students complained about bitterly.)

The book traverses the breadth of the interior of North India, from dusty second-tier cities to dusty towns to a prestigious colonial-era university. Poonam spends much of her time in Ranchi, where she grew up, a small city of around one million people in north-eastern India, the capital of the resource-rich state of Jharkhand. She also travels to Indore, Meerut and Allahabad, all cities with markers of second-tier aspiration and modernity: "airport, apartment complexes, token chain-brand hotel, token shopping mall", and so too traffic, pollution, crime and sewage.

Globalisation is a central theme of the book. The opening chapter presents a compelling representation of this: a profile of WittyFeed, a BuzzFeed-style viral content company headquartered in the central Indian city of Indore. Founded in 2014, it now gets about 250 million page views per month. Those who work there have rarely travelled outside North India, but pride themselves on having cracked the code of what makes Americans click, engendering a newfound confidence of their grasp of the inner workings of distant minds.

Anger emerges as another theme. Poonam focuses on interviews with a handful of twenty-somethings, including a low-caste milkman turned English teacher, a regional radio DJ and an aspiring right-wing politician with views rooted in Hindu ideology. Only one, a student activist politician, is a woman. The rest are men, a reflection of the gender composition seen on your average North Indian regional streetscape, where, unlike in other parts of India, women from the middle and upper classes are rarely seen (those who can afford it stay at home, and travel by car when they do venture out).

Poonam's status as a Ranchi-born, Delhi-dwelling Hindi speaker confers upon her a special position that allows her access to such stories. She is inside but outside; one of "us" but now from a different world. Her book does what so many others that purport to draw the definitive picture of contemporary India do not: it tells the story from the inside out. She does this by finding stories from deep within the inner reaches of India, both geographically and figuratively. She finds young men whose sole purpose in life, as they tell it, is to beat up couples on Valentine's Day, considering the concept of romantic love an affront to traditional Hindu values. Another man is a cow protector who, along with carloads of compatriots, trawls the highways at night looking for people – Muslims – working in the cattle trade, to beat them up – or worse.

As Poonam writes of one character: "Arjun Kumar is what think pieces explaining the Trump and Brexit verdicts term a loser of globalization, one of the millions of leftover youths whose anger is transforming world politics. It's like the world swept past him while he was arranging chairs in the Bajrang Dal office. Kumar is not sure he will find a job he'd like or find a girl who'd like him. On an elemental level, he doesn't know if he matters to the world. There's only one way left for him to make that happen: punish everyone who's moved ahead of him in that queue."

What ties all the characters – in particular, the young men – is their deep desire for *izzat*: honour, prestige, reputation. In this generation, the desire for *izzat* is primordial, binding together the traditions from their feudal village past with the shining, privileged future they know to be out there for them if they just hustle hard enough.

I can recognise this craving in my bribe-wielding student. He might already have money, a degree of status and be on the way to some power, but he is still on the hustle. And if that means faking an Ayn Rand essay on the road to *izzat*, then so be it. Poonam's book might be subtitled "how young Indians are changing the world", but this is perhaps an ironic take, as many of Poonam's scenarios describe pitiable circumstances and characters who are striving against the odds yet hurling themselves against an impenetrable wall, built of personal circumstances and global factors. Yet Indians are resilient, and while Poonam's dreamers might be better described as "the disappointed", their unbridled hope and enthusiasm is laudable. If India could just create those twelve million jobs each year, it might allow the hopes and dreams of its young people to continue to flicker.

Aarti Betigeri

The Death of Truth
Michiko Kakutani
William Collins

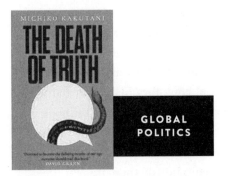

GLOBAL
POLITICS

For an obituary, this is a disturbingly slender book. I looked at it askance for days, unopened on my desk: could the truth be dispatched in around 160 pages (plus notes)? If Michiko Kakutani, well-known former book critic for *The New York Times*, in possession of a Pulitzer Prize for Criticism, can kill it off with such apparent ease, with a flick of the pen, why has it been so hard to nail down all these years?

She dedicates the book to "journalists everywhere working to report the news". But somehow I wasn't convinced by this lofty dedication. Seeking reassurance, I turned to Google Scholar and searched for "truth and journalism": there were 525,000 results. On top of the list rested a journal article by the prolific media scholar Silvio Waisbord about fake news called "Truth Is What Happens to News". Among his observations: "Conventional notions of news and truth that ground standard journalistic practice are harder to achieve and maintain amid the destabilization of the past hierarchical order."

Later, Waisbord cites Mersault's famous counsel in Camus' *The Outsider:* "everything is true and nothing is true". Together, these observations didn't make me feel much better.

A few days later, I sat down to write a blurb for an event on public broadcasting. When I stumbled, hesitated and eventually expunged the word "expert" to describe both the ABC's news director Gaven Morris and *The Australian*'s columnist Judith Sloan (a former ABC deputy chair), I silently cursed Michael Gove, the MP and Brexiteer, and realised I could resist no longer. People, as Gove claimed, may have had "enough of experts". But perhaps they could handle a short dose of the "truth" about truth. I opened the book.

Kakutani's primary target in *The Death of Truth* is obvious – his name is Trump, and he is the embodiment of what ails much of the world's political discourse. Kakutani describes him as a "larger than life, over-the-top avatar of narcissism, mendacity, ignorance, prejudice, boorishness, demagoguery, and tyrannical impulses". The Troller-in-Chief infects most chapters, is name-checked every few pages and is painted as either a harbinger of a new totalitarianism or the apotheosis of the post-truth era.

Kakutani opens with Hannah Arendt: "The ideal subject of totalitarian rule is not the convinced Nazi or the convinced Communist, but people for whom the distinction between fact and fiction ... between true and false ... no longer exist." She ends by citing the US founding fathers: Jefferson, Washington and, most succinctly, Madison: "A popular Government, without acquiring popular information, or the means of acquiring it, is but a Prologue to a Farce or a Tragedy; or perhaps both."

Between the two quotes, and true to her calling as a literary critic, Kakutani enlists a steady stream of polemicists, journalists, commentators, historians and academics. This makes the book both a biography of truth's demise and an extended and sophisticated meditation on these fraught times. Aside from Arendt, who pops up frequently, she cites Orwell, Wolfe, Roth, Yeats, Pynchon – even Kipling and T.S. Eliot. There are moments when the use of the literary canon feels a bit showy. Okay, you've read a lot of books, Michiko; we get it.

Here, she gets to unload on a subject I suspect has been annoying her for years: postmodernism. That is, the idea that everything is relative and open to deconstruction, and so nothing holds solid meaning.

These parts of the book – and her excoriation of a culture more interested in feelings than facts – make for the most interesting and rewarding reading. Shooting Trump is, in the hands of a progressive East Coast intellectual, akin to drowning reality TV stars in a vat of lights and make-up; taking down Club Derrida, and skilfully charting how the curse of relativism, the narcissistic attenuations of identity politics and the march of the cultural wars jumping from the left to the right are much bigger achievements. This is what makes *The Death of Truth* so confronting – because you might well read this and conclude, "It's my own fault."

While Kakutani sets up her stall on the White House lawn, exposing the truth-decaying ethos of the Trump era, this is not best understood as a political work. It is a social, cultural and historical travelogue. And the final destination is, well, looking at us in the mirror. Have we been far too prepared to accept that "everything ha[s] an infinitude of meanings" and is corrupted by the author's point of view, gender, social standing, education, heritage and so on? That,

"in short, there [i]s no such thing as truth"? No more agreed-upon facts; it's all up for grabs – and my facts are as good as yours.

In several well-crafted passages, Kakutani cleverly jumps us back from her attacks on smarty-pants intellectuals and a society obsessed with "moi" and subjectivity (at the expense of society and objectivity) to Trump. Norman Vincent Peale, the author of 1952's self-help bestseller *The Power of Positive Thinking*, is cited as an early influence on the forty-fifth president via his father, Fred Trump. Peale writes, "Any fact facing us, however difficult, even seemingly hopeless, is not so important as our attitude toward that fact."

That was written more than seventy years ago; the death of truth has been a long time coming. In fact, there are few points in time since the end of World War II that aren't enlisted to Kakutani's case. In this way, the work is like one of the maps found in the back of in-flight magazines: all the loopy red lines, of differing lengths, reaching the same destination, named Decline o' Reason. Again, the literary greats are called upon to show us the way.

Roth and Wolfe are employed to cajole and extol action and embrace the world beyond the self or, as Wolfe wrote in 1989, to "head out into this wild, bizarre, unpredictable, Hog-stomping Baroque country of ours and reclaim it as literary property". This is one of a few points where Kakutani gets close to directly criticising journalism. The implication: if only reporters had talked to more "hog-stompers", they might have better picked the election of Trump. In other words, dear reporter, leave the beltway, get off Twitter and go talk to the real people.

But that's about the extent of Kakutani's critique of the fourth estate. Fake news, internet trolls, Russian manipulation, technological distractions and social media platforms happen to it and around it. Journalism soldiers on, seeking the truth, toting up Trump's lies (5.9 a day in the first year), getting beaten up – but comes across as incapable of winning the war, at least alone. Fair enough: it's a tall mountain to climb. As Waisbord writes, "journalism as a single institution cannot possibly control this environment".

Yet hard as it may be, Kakutani's sparkling prose and bright intellect falters on how to resuscitate truth. She is convincing on how we got here, less assured as to how we might get back. Perhaps it is beyond the remit of the book, which is largely spent listing the multiple usurpers of truth. Is journalism practised in good faith a vital part of the resistance? Yes, of course. But is this enough? No. To my mind, journalism needs to spend as much time working out the demand side of the equation – what do readers want, what will they buy and why? – as it does on ensuring the bona fides of supply. This may well be another book. Kakutani's work is definitely not it. She leaves us with some simple nostrums: "There are no easy remedies, but it's essential that citizens defy the cynicism and resignation that autocrats and power-hungry politicians depend upon to subvert resistance."

Perhaps the book that needs to be written should be called *Truth: Its Demise and How to Bring It Back to Life*. Such a publication would benefit from fewer references to the literary canon and more attention on the leading role that journalists, editors, publishers, digital platforms and their audiences need to play in

resurrecting the truth. Hmm, I'd love to read, or even write, it.

Peter Fray

Will China Save the Planet?
Barbara Finamore
Polity Press

China's breakneck growth, first unleashed during the 1980s, was once synonymous with environmental unsustainability. As Barbara Finamore writes in *Will China Save the Planet?*, a government accounting exercise found that widespread pollution of China's air, water and soil caused losses of over US$80 billion in 2004, equivalent to about 3 per cent of China's GDP that year.

China is also the world's largest greenhouse-gas emitter by volume, and its environmental reputation hit an infamous low point in late 2009, when the country was widely blamed for the collapse of UN-led climate talks in Copenhagen.

Yet since then, China's star has risen markedly. At the Paris conference in late 2015, nearly 200 countries signed a historic agreement to limit the global average temperature rise to well below 2 degrees Celsius. As Finamore rightly points out, China was "widely credited with playing a constructive role in reaching" the agreement, particularly through the unprecedented joint announcement of emissions curbs the previous year by Chinese president Xi Jinping and his then counterpart, US president Barack Obama.

Following the 2016 election of Donald Trump – who has dismantled environmental regulation in the United States, committed to withdraw from Paris and, preposterously, even called climate change a Chinese hoax – President Xi has only doubled down on his support for the UN accord and a low-carbon transition. At the 19th Congress of the Chinese Communist Party in October 2017, President Xi said that China was in the "driving seat" when it comes to "international cooperation" on climate change.

So is China really stepping up to a position of global leadership on climate? Finamore's answer, in this concise and accessible volume, seems a cautious yes.

Yet while the credit for this, in Finamore's book and elsewhere, has largely gone to China's leaders, much should also be attributed to the role of ordinary people, entrepreneurs and grassroots environmental activists, whose freedom of action has often been severely constrained.

The author correctly identifies self-interest at the heart of China's turnaround, pointing not only to the Chinese government's concerns about the country's climate-change vulnerabilities, but also to its drive to curb air pollution, to mollify mounting domestic concern about environmental degradation, to burnish its soft power and to lead in clean energy – the "largest new market opportunity of the twenty-first century". This means, of course, dethroning "King Coal", and Finamore, an environmental lawyer and campaigner with decades of experience in China, doesn't make light of the challenge. Coal's share in power generation in China may have dropped from 80 per cent in 2010 to 60 per cent in 2017, but it's still a tough dependence to break – and, like anywhere else, there is also the pushback from "those who benefit from smokestack industries or stand to lose under the 'new normal': displaced workers, local governments, and the coal industry itself". Still, Finamore makes a convincing case that the sheer dynamism of the renewable energy industry will win out. In 2017 alone, she notes, China installed more solar capacity than the total, cumulative solar capacity of any other country as of the end of 2016 – or enough photovoltaic panels to cover a soccer field every hour. The scale of Chinese manufacturing, meanwhile, has had a global effect, driving down solar prices "faster than anyone had ever imagined".

The book also discusses innovation in the wind power and green buildings industries, but its profile of China's electric vehicle industry – an important sector to examine, given the government's ambition to compete globally in the electric car market – overlooks an important player in the nation's energy transformation: its people. Finamore's top-down narrative, which serves to valorise the state-led, centrally managed transition in China, rightly draws attention to the government's decision to single out electric vehicles as a strategic priority. But a combination of factors, including the challenge of scaling charging infrastructure and grid integration, has proven difficult and helped to stifle consumer demand for EVs. Meanwhile, the humble electric bicycle – a demand-led, street-level game-changer – has become ubiquitous in Chinese cities, despite being actively discouraged by government policy (many cities still ban them). Overlooked in this volume, as it is by Chinese policymakers, the e-bike is cheap to purchase, doesn't need expensive charging infrastructure, helps to solve urban air pollution – and, crucially, illustrates the ways that China's bottom-up innovation and entrepreneurship, which it has in spades, can be unleashed to address environmental and social problems.

Moreover, exploring the role of China's grassroots efforts would draw attention to a darker side of its changing political context, which receives short shrift in the text. Finamore notes that environmental enforcement in China was improved in 2015 through amendments to its *Environmental Protection Law*, which gave NGOs the ability to bring legal action against polluters. But she overlooks new laws restricting civil society, including 2017 legislation that put foreign groups under the supervision of the security services – and has sent an icy chill through the NGO sector.

Grassroots environmentalism flourished in China over the last decade, with the formation of hundreds of thousands of registered groups, and many more operating unregistered. Chinese civil society recorded several victories in opposing environmentally damaging projects, such as large dams and proposed petrochemical plants. But the past five years has seen steadily tightening controls on information, universities and think tanks, and severe restrictions on access to justice. This is critical, not only given the continued environmental challenges at home, but also the urgency of curbing China's overseas investments in polluting sectors. Through President Xi's signature overseas investment plan, the Belt and Road Initiative (BRI), surplus capital and technology is likely to continue to flow from industries such as coal, steel and cement, where production is slowing in China, into emerging economies.

Finamore does discuss the need to improve the environmental sustainability standards of China's overseas investments – and rightly flags the stalwart efforts of green-leaning reformers in the banking system. But with much investment proposed for new coal-generation capacity overseas, the BRI already stands to lock in high carbon growth, presenting a critical challenge for the two-degree target under the Paris Agreement.

The question posed by the title, therefore, is salient – and the opportunities afforded by China's expansion into the clean energy sector are potentially huge – but realities on the ground warrant a tempering of Finamore's optimism, both over China, as civil society faces a clampdown, and overseas, as the country's environmental footprint expands rapidly.

Sam Geall

Dictatorland: The Men Who Stole Africa
Paul Kenyon
Head of Zeus

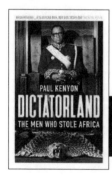

Paul Kenyon describes *Dictatorland* as the story of "how a whole continent has been robbed in broad daylight ... and the story of the men who stole Africa".

As the sensationalist title and description indicate, the book perpetuates generalisations about Africa that have long coloured Western media coverage of the continent. Kenyon, a veteran BBC correspondent, spent years reporting from Africa and boasts of having visited almost every African country in trailing the footsteps of these men. On this basis, he considers himself qualified to claim that some of Africa's worst dictators singlehandedly plundered an entire continent.

It is a bold assertion, which demonstrates how little such grandiose statements are interrogated when the story is about Africa. Would the same be said about Europe's dictators – would they be blamed for the entire continent's woes? Would all European countries be lumped into one convenient narrative that negates their diversity, the nuances in their cultures and politics? I think few would try to get away with oversimplifying the histories of those nations to fit a catchy headline. But why doesn't that apply to reporting on Africa?

Much Western media coverage about the continent seems fixated on a singular narrative of Africa – that of a place of poverty, disease and conflict. This narrative is reinforced through a series of myths and stereotypes.

One persistent falsehood involves treating an entire continent as a country. *Dictatorland* briefly details the political environments in the seven countries it focuses on: the Democratic Republic of the Congo, Zimbabwe, Libya, Nigeria, Equatorial Guinea, Côte d'Ivoire and Eritrea. Yet it connects individual scenarios to a story of a failing continent, suggesting simplistically that a handful of greedy long-serving rulers are to blame for its alleged demise. Africa is made up of some fifty-four countries, each diverse. The case studies Kenyon uses are based in different geographical regions, with unique languages and religious, ethnic, racial and colonial histories, yet the reader rarely gets a sense of this differentiation.

The book also rarely considers the role these factors play in the politics of individual countries. For example, the Democratic Republic of the Congo and Libya share commonalities in having endured long-serving leaders – Mobutu Sese Seko and Muammar Gaddafi – but that is where the similarities end. The Congo was for more than seventy years controlled by Belgium, which, under pressure from other European nations, reluctantly handed power to the traditional owners (among whom, according to historians, were only four people with a tertiary education, and minimal experience in managing institutions – the Belgians set the Congo up to fail from the beginning). Libya, meanwhile, was ruled by the Persians, the Greeks and the Egyptians, and eventually became part of the Roman Empire and an early centre of Christianity, before invasions brought Islam to the area.

Dictatorland reinforces another myth about the continent: that it is static, not evolving and developing. In reality, Africa's population of more than a billion people includes a sizeable and rapidly growing middle class, which is of increasing economic significance. While poverty persists in parts of the continent, that's not the full picture. The United Nations estimates that the working-age population will triple to 1.3 billion by 2050 in Sub-Saharan Africa; in North Africa, this figure is expected to be more than 1.5 billion. GDP growth in Sub-Saharan African countries in recent years has exceeded the average of emerging and developing countries.

That myth ties into another: that the history of the continent

began once the colonisers left. The history of Africa dates back hundreds of thousands of years. The book's failure to contextualise modern Africa with its pre-colonial past reinforces these other falsehoods. It means that Africans are viewed as "uncivilised" and "primitive" even when history tells us that the oldest civilisations can be traced back to this landmass. It is against this narrative that Africa is cast as the "hopeless" and "helpless" continent. *Dictatorland* fails to see an Africa in which Africans find solutions to African problems and are not waiting to be "saved".

Every tragedy needs its villains, and in this story the seven leaders singled out are riddled with all the clichés that have dogged discourse about Africa in the West for decades, at least since Joseph Conrad's *Heart of Darkness*, casting Africans as brutes and savages who can't govern on their own. The selected figures – Zimbabwe's Robert Mugabe (who ruled from 1980 to 2017), Libya's Muammar Gaddafi (1969–2011), Nigeria's Sani Abacha (1993–1998), the Democratic Republic of the Congo's Mobutu Sese Seko (1965–1997), Nigeria's Sani

Abacha (1993–1998), Côte d'Ivoire's Felix Houphuet-Boigny (1960–1993), Equatorial Guinea's Obiang Nguema (since 1979) and Eritrea's Isaias Afwerki (since 1993) – fit the "colourful" and "exotic" narrative of the stereotypical African dictator. The cover captures the most flamboyant of them: Sese Seko, who is pictured adorned in European-style military attire with a leopard-skin rug at his feet as he stares at the camera.

The book does highlight the complicity of Western governments in supporting these leaders and overlooking human-rights abuses. But this is limited to post-colonial analysis, as though that is the extent of European involvement on the African continent. It glosses over the horrific killings and abuses that European governments have committed on this resource-rich continent, their failure to develop the countries they were pillaging and their reluctant handover of control, without equipping the local populations to manage these countries according to legal, commercial and scientific systems designed by the Europeans themselves. It neglects to examine the impact that the carving up of the continent at the Berlin Conference in 1884 and 1885 had on inter-ethnic relations and how that continues to affect contemporary politics.

To understand the present, we must understand the past. These persistent myths have origins deeply rooted in colonialism and were used by colonial authorities and institutions (including the media) to maintain white supremacy and domination. Despite colonialism ending almost half a century ago, few in contemporary Western media organisations have sought to consider how their coverage of the African continent continues to perpetuate these ideas.

As the late Nigerian writer Chinua Achebe once proclaimed, "The whole idea of the stereotype is to simplify." Africa is more than the clichés and stereotypes. The Western media's failure to see that is a failure to see a modern, diverse continent that continues to thrive and is waiting for the rest of the world's perceptions to catch up.

Santilla Chingaipe

Correspondence

"Dangerous Proximity"
by Michael Wesley

Jim Molan

Michael Wesley's essay in AFA4: *Defending Australia*, "Dangerous Proximity", is a pleasure to read. However, some of his judgements are made too confidently, and some internal contradictions in the piece are confusing.

Michael's article is a reminder that for decades Australia has lacked a national security strategy beyond hoping that a "great and powerful friend" will come to the rescue in the event of conflict. In retrospect, this approach worked. But I agree that it is no longer viable when the Indo-Pacific is emerging as one of the most important theatres of great power competition.

The United States is no longer the supreme global military power it was – on this I think Michael and I agree. A series of global circumstances – fifteen years of acute conflict in the Middle East; eight years of Obama; seven years of sequestration; the rise of China, Russia, Iran and North Korea – plus the failure of US allies to maintain adequate military capability means that Australia had better prepare to look after itself.

The US military strategy behind which Australia shelters was structured, staffed, equipped, paid for and operated to simultaneously win two big wars and one little war. Today, with a bit of luck, the US military might just be able to win one big war. Yet the US National Security Strategy identifies its challengers as "four nations and an ideology" (Russia, Iran, China, North Korea and Islamic extremism), which are unlikely to be politely hostile one at a time.

Australia's relationship with our Asian neighbours must change, but given that such change will be limited by our values and interests, Australia may find itself needing to defend those values against a range of threats, as we are doing at this very moment.

Any consideration of Australia's defence in a contested Asia must acknowledge that it is both US intent and capability that is forcing change. It is because every US ally from the Baltic, through the Gulf, to the Indian Ocean and the Pacific wants the United States to come to its aid, exactly as Australia does, that the United States no longer has the capability to assist everywhere.

Michael's contention that Australia "has lost its technological edge" is hard to justify. The edge might be lessening, but I cannot agree that we have lost it. The problem is not just the technological sophistication of the ADF, but also its size. The overarching problem remains the lack of a national security strategy. Such a strategy would highlight that our defence force is far too small, with no reserves of key equipment, weapons or ammunition; a frightening lack of resilience in many of the civilian support functions, such as energy and liquid fuel; and absolutely no modern mobilisation plans. An enemy may not even need coercive diplomacy. While I accept what Michael says about change to the ADF, that should be determined by a national security strategy, not by our musings.

In the past, Australia could get away with small forces structured to support our allies. Now we need to define not just our forces, but also our society, on the basis of a national security strategy that accepts war as a real possibility. I suspect that a rational strategy will demand Australia's military forces be larger, more technologically advanced and provided for by our own society and industrial base. Then we can redefine our international relations in accordance with our values, and maybe even talk about operational concepts and tactics.

Michael judges that "direct military attack has taken a back seat to coercive statecraft". I wish I could be that certain about modern warfare. The equally (if not more) likely probability is that future conflict will feature coercive diplomacy intermixed with economic pressure and cyber aggression aimed at diminishing national resilience with a view to a form of Finlandisation. If that does not achieve the aggressor's aims, high-technology war will follow. Coercive diplomacy and cyber are not substitutes for kinetics – they can be a prelude to it.

All such actions can still be deterred, but only by a nation that can "win" in a conflict and do so decisively. Australia should be able to defeat any threat against it, but at the moment it would take a ridiculously long time to realise its amazing defence potential. And time is likely to be the one thing we do not have.

I agree with Michael that our "approaches to defence planning are inadequate", but there should be a rule in commentary such as ours: no comment is to be made about tactical issues, in which we are all brilliant, until we actually have a national security strategy.

Jim Molan, Liberal Senator for New South Wales and former major general in the Australian Army

---

Michael Shoebridge

There's much to admire in Michael Wesley's hypothesis in his essay "Dangerous Proximity" – the historical sweep, encompassing the British settlement in Australia; strategists obsessed with how to defend a continent of few people; the changing nature of conflict through the advent of technology; and the rise of "coercive statecraft". I came away disturbed and motivated. Australia, it seems, needs to completely rethink its approach to security because the nature and purpose of force has been transformed, and armed conflict is not the only way to defeat an opponent.

Wesley argues that long-range bombardment and nuclear weapons make major combat between powerful countries unthinkable. A new statecraft, based on coercive control and influence, lowers the risk of a nuclear exchange. Long-range precision-guided hypersonic missiles are being acquired by Russia, China, India and other Asian nations. Australia has lost its technological edge and the benefits of its remote location. Worse, new weapons threatening the Malacca Strait will see ships sailing around the east and south of Australia – placing us in the heart of "competition among the United States, China, India and Japan for influence in South-East Asia and the South Pacific".

Most concerning of all, Wesley says that the US alliance will be of little use, as its logic has shifted worryingly in the face of deepening Sino–US rivalry. Australia might need to come to US aid in a war with China, and it's no longer inevitable that the United States will have the capacity to help Australia in conflict. Australia may have to resist coercive statecraft from China or other powers alone, and may have to defend our huge continent without a technological edge and without American assistance.

I don't buy this. Some of the big assumptions Wesley makes aren't just shaky – they're wrong. He's right that US military power relative to China's is decreasing, but this does not mean that the United States won't be able to help us in a war with China. Nuclear weapons remain key to containing, and preventing, such confrontations, and the alliance means protection by the nuclear-armed Americans. Military conflict between powerful states is not "unthinkable". It's precisely *because* the United States is willing to use nuclear weapons in a conflict with China or any other major power that it possesses the ability to deter them from going to war.

Any calculation by Beijing that it could attack Australia, Japan or South Korea without risking nuclear war with the United States is erroneous, as history and key current US planning documents make clear. As in the Cold War, the risks of assuming that the United States won't use nuclear weapons are so grave that Beijing is unlikely to take the bet. Let's not talk ourselves or the United States out of the benefits of extended deterrence – let's work with the United States to strengthen it as the regional order changes and technology evolves.

Wesley is right that China and other powers are exercising "coercive statecraft" rather than engaging in direct conflict. That isn't new – there was a lot of it in the Cold War and even in Roman times. But its utility is reducing as targets become more aware and better at responding – individually and collectively. We've seen pushback against Beijing and Moscow, such as cancelled Belt and Road Initiative deals that would leave unpayable debts, and the exposure of covert interference, from the Skripal poisoning to cyber intrusions. We're seeing international cooperation to counter military aggression in Eastern Europe and in Asia, along with sunlight on predatory deals that cede decision-making to other powers.

In our region, beyond naval forces to counter maritime grey-zone activities, the capabilities for resisting coercion are not military. They are political, economic, counterintelligence and cyber tools – which all require investment and the will to use.

I also don't buy the emergence of a shipping route around Australia because of security fears over the Malacca Strait. In peacetime, no company will divert ships thousands of kilometres around the bottom of the world – economics sends shipping along lines of least cost, which is why so many vessels will continue through the Malacca Strait. While in a major war shipping may well go around Australia, such a change would not occur before the outbreak of conflict. And then, Australia would not be working alone to protect shipping lines.

Even if I'm wrong about China not being deterred by US capabilities, or about a southern shipping route opening up, I challenge anyone to describe the circumstances of a major confrontation with China that involves Australia but not our Asian security partners – notably Indonesia, Vietnam, Japan and South Korea – and the United States. China moving forces to attack Australia or showering us with missiles in a conflict between only the two countries seems a scenario that even Wesley has difficulty conjuring convincingly, yet it apparently requires us to entirely rethink our defences.

An important point on which I agree with Wesley is that Australia's technological edge is eroding because of the rise of Asian – notably Chinese – military and civil technologies. The United States faces the same challenge. This requires profound rethinking of our defence concepts and working with Asian, US and European partners to protect our and the region's security.

It's unlikely that the force structure outlined in the 2009 and 2016 Defence White Papers – to be pieced together slowly up to the mid-2050s, when the last of twelve 'future submarines' turns up – is the answer to looming technological and strategic change. A force structure designed in 1894 would not have been useful when World War II erupted in 1939.

The challenge is for Australia to understand how to work strategically with partners such as Japan, Indonesia, Vietnam and India to ensure our collective security. This will require an entirely new approach to our relationships with these countries.

There's also a profound need to conceive of an ADF force design to cope with technological shifts, so it is resilient to adversaries that have weapons, systems and sensors that either match Australia's, are superior or are sufficiently different to produce surprise during combat. This includes systems such as advanced missiles and sensors, weapons enabled by artificial intelligence, cyber capabilities, space systems, and air, sea and land platforms. The ADF's force design will need to be tailored to work with partners to resist coercion from the South Pacific to the South China Sea.

Unlike Wesley, however, I believe that all of this work will be done best by understanding and continuing to invest in the power of the US–Australia alliance – guided by Australia's national interests.

Michael Shoebridge, director of defence and strategy at
the Australian Strategic Policy Institute

Michael Wesley responds

Jim Molan and Michael Shoebridge have each thought deeply, for a long time, about the challenges of defending Australia. Molan has served this country in uniform and has faced the rapidly evolving nature of warfare and coercion firsthand. Shoebridge's long and distinguished career in the Department of Defence has given him a decisive role in shaping the evolution of Australia's strategic policy.

Both commentators take issue with contradictions and assumptions in my essay, but seem to spend a lot of time agreeing with me.

Molan observes that the relative decline of American military power to the point where it "might just be able to win one big war" poses real challenges for an Australian defence policy centred on an alliance with the United States. He rightly points out that we are not alone in this; the United States has a range of allies expecting it to come to their help in extremis, but at a time of multiple challenges to the international status quo, there are real questions over its capacity and willingness to do so.

While Molan challenges my assertion that Australia has lost its technological edge, he goes on to add that things are made even worse by the small size of our armed forces and our lack of reserves. His call for a national security strategy raises more questions than it answers. Would this supersede the current Defence White Paper? Would it be akin to the Gillard government's 2013 National Security Strategy? And how would it define our society, as he suggests it should?

Shoebridge takes issue with my pessimism about the Australia–United States alliance. Perhaps he's right, but he makes some heroic assumptions in mounting his case. He states, "It's precisely *because* the United States is willing to use nuclear weapons in a conflict with China or any other major power that it possesses the ability to deter them from going to war." And again, "As in the Cold War, the risks of assuming that the United States won't use nuclear weapons are so grave that Beijing is unlikely to take the bet." He needs to take another look at the history of the Cold War. In three military confrontations with China – the Korean War (1950–53) and the First (1954–55) and Second (1958) Taiwan Strait Crises – the United States did not use nuclear weapons against China, despite Beijing attacking close Washington allies and interests. This was at a time when China had no nuclear weapons. The United States had nuclear weapons, but it did not deter China from challenging American interests in Asia. The same pattern occurred during the Vietnam War. I'm not sure why Shoebridge thinks that China will be more compelled by the US nuclear threat now that Beijing has around 260 warheads capable of launching devastating counterstrikes on the US homeland.

Shoebridge also suggests that coercive statecraft is becoming less effective as targets become more aware and better at responding. I would like to be that sanguine, but it appears to me that technological developments are opening up new avenues of coercive statecraft. As our parliamentary battles over encryption legislation show, we're playing catch-up constantly. Simply assuming we've worked it out seems to be a recipe for the worst kind of strategic surprise.

Shoebridge's optimism is again on show in relation to the South Pacific. He doubts that in peacetime companies would divert ships thousands of kilometres. I agree. But strategy is not about planning for peace; it's about planning for war. Naval bases are used to protect shipping in waters that could become contested in periods of conflict. This is a very old principle captured pithily by American maritime strategist Alfred Thayer Mahan, who is required reading in the Chinese Navy's senior ranks. The basic facts of a battle in the Pacific are: none of the major Asian combatants is self-sufficient in energy, so any war strategy should be based around blockading their ability to resupply; and the easiest routes to blockade are through South-East Asia, so other routes, and the safety of shipping through them, will come into play. Therefore, a key element of planning for future scenarios, it seems to me, might be to develop a presence in the South Pacific.

I'm unsure why Shoebridge assumes that I'm only thinking of a scenario in which Australia alone is subject to Chinese coercion. I'm not. That's why I discuss the need to build close defence relationships with other Asian security partners, a point on which, at least, he seems to agree.

Michael Wesley, dean of the College of Asia
and the Pacific at the Australian National University

"A Nuclear-armed Australia"
by Stephan Frühling

Alison Broinowski

ntellectual preoccupations come and go. "Transparency and account-ability", once widely recommended, now rarely figure in the discourse. "Globalisation" and "governance" have recently yielded top place as the most overused expressions in foreign affairs to "the international rules-based order". This latest buzz-phrase – featured in last issue's Back Page section – is more often cited than applied, particularly by Australian governments. It means different things to different people: to economists it's the Bretton Woods institutions; to lawyers and diplomats it's the international legal system, repeated appeals to which count for less and less. Even rationalism, the orderly emblem of the Enlightenment, is being overruled by rules-free Trumpery, Michiko Kakutani argues in *The Death of Truth: Notes on Falsehood in the Age of Trump*. So it's surprising that Stephan Frühling should refer to another "new world order", a phrase that was on everyone's lips in the years of President George H.W. Bush, but that hardly applies to today's disorderly world.

Equally unexpected is Associate Professor Frühling's reference to a "nascent debate" about Australia acquiring nuclear weapons. This debate must be taking place quietly inside our proliferating national security establishment, for it is not audible in the wider community. Occasional expressions of enthusiasm are heard from those with vested interests in Australia developing nuclear power plants, but these voices never raise nuclear weapons. If plans exist for our future submarine fleet to be nuclear-powered or nuclear-armed, the government has not taken the risk of revealing them, nor what their eye-watering cost to our "debt and deficit" would be. When Australia's ICAN won the latest Nobel Peace Prize for its promotion of the Treaty on the Prohibition of Nuclear

Weapons, many outside the major parties were delighted. If Australians want nuclear weapons, Frühling's article is the first many of them will have heard of it.

Frühling's account of Australia's on and off, past and prospective, nuclear involvement is useful, if necessarily selective. It is salutary to be reminded that ever-eager Australian defence planners sought to enable the new F-111s to carry nuclear weapons, and that they were again considered for Australia following China's first atomic test of 1964. But Australians remember vividly the British nuclear tests at Maralinga, whose dreadful consequences Frühling fails to mention. He omits Australia's efforts over many years to achieve nuclear non-proliferation and disarmament and to eliminate nuclear testing. He does not discuss Canberra's current bipartisan about-face, refusing to ban atomic weapons, even though it could back his argument that Australia should consider acquiring an independent nuclear capability. He refers repeatedly to Australia having to get American permission to build our own nuclear weapons but does not explain how or when Australia incurred this obligation. Safe reprocessing and disposal of Australia's nuclear waste he ignores entirely.

Frühling cogently sets out the possible nuclear and conventional threats to Australia and methodically eliminates all of them, apart from speculating about a future powerful Indonesia. Yet he persists in arguing the case for nuclear weapons, which he says could substitute for conventional forces or complement them, and could have small warheads for short-range "tactical" purposes, particularly in "maritime battle", to safeguard the sea and air approaches to Australia. Would such restraint, and a "spiked moat" around our continent (as Frühling puts it), deter Australia's neighbours from responding with an arms race and nuclear weapons of their choice? Would Asian nations with which we need closer and deeper relations (as the October 2012 "Australia in the Asian Century" White Paper argued) trust Australia not to aim our nuclear devices at them? It seems unlikely. Moreover, the more countries have them, the greater the risk that nuclear weapons will be used, accidentally or by design.

The main arguments for and against nuclear weapons, which don't appear in Frühling's article, are economic, legal, environmental and ethical. Even for a country such as Australia, which has uranium, the costs of developing nuclear power and nuclear weapons from scratch are crippling, economically distorting and not feasible. Any country that has signed the Nuclear Non-Proliferation

Treaty would be in breach if it built or used nuclear weapons, and could face international sanctions. A country that threatens or uses conventional force against another state that is not directly attacking it is in breach of international law, and its leaders could be accused of the war crime of aggression. A country that causes a nuclear attack releases deadly radiation over a wide area, rendering it uninhabitable even for the humans, animals and plants that survive, and a counter-attack compounds the disaster. A country whose leaders can force others to suffer "what they must" – as Frühling cites the ancient Athenians doing to the Melians – should first consider treating others as they wish to be treated.

Frühling is careful not to prescribe nuclear arms for Australia, and instead sets out our strategic options, suggesting that they deserve timely consideration in the context of an unreliable US alliance. Independence has never been more desirable. But before Australians seek security in nuclear weapons, we should remember Ronald Reagan's wisest words, with which Mikhail Gorbachev agreed: "Nuclear war cannot be won and must never be fought." Australia should remind others of them at every opportunity.

Alison Broinowski, former Australian diplomat and academic, and vice-president of Honest History and of Australians for War Powers Reform

Paul Bracken

S
tephan Frühling poses a controversial question: whether Australia should get its own nuclear weapons. He answers that the security environment is changing so much that the prospect cannot be dismissed out of hand, as it has been for many decades. Given this, we must think through the consequences in clear-eyed fashion, he says. What would an Australian nuclear weapon mean for proliferation? Would it make Australia a target for attack by China in some future crisis? These are good questions, and raising them is an indication of how much the Asian security environment is changing.

Underlying his analysis is the return of great power rivalry. And this leads to a larger strategic problem, which goes beyond Australian security. It is *the* important question of our time: what role will nuclear weapons play in major power rivalry? International politics and technology suggest that their role will be substantial.

But perhaps nuclear weapons will play little or no role. Cyber, drones, AI, hypersonic missiles and so on might obviate the need for nuclear weapons and shift the locus of competition to these technologies.

Many writings about cyber and advanced technologies seem to make this case, because they essentially ignore nuclear weapons altogether, or suggest that they are "confined" to a very small box of remote possibilities. They may be needed, this argument goes, but only in highly unlikely and largely unimaginable circumstances.

This view of nuclear weapons in major power rivalry is highly appealing. If we must have nuclear weapons, it offers a way to minimise their impact. An answer might look like this. Suppose each major power (the United States,

Russia and China) had 100 secure, protected second-strike weapons. Nuclear weapons could then be eliminated from the rivalry because there would be no benefit to getting more of them. If a country were to do so, the action would be met immediately, by other major powers responding in kind.

The problem with this perspective is that it narrowly frames the problem of what nuclear "use" really means. Because the lesson of the first nuclear age, the Cold War, is that *you don't have to fire a nuclear weapon to use it.* There are nuclear head games, as Richard Nixon's "madman" behaviour showed during the Vietnam War. The Cuban Missile Crisis alerts, brinksmanship, deterrent posturing in the Taiwan crisis, the US maritime strategy in the 1980s and the Pershing missile threat to destroy Moscow command centres all "used" nuclear weapons. The purpose was to scare the other side, as with maritime attacks that could destroy a high fraction of a protected second-strike submarine force – the US maritime strategy of the 1980s.

Nuclear weapons were also used for easy rhetorical threats, and to signal anger, if not much else. And they were used for defence on the cheap, to cut expensive conventional forces.

Also, they were used for enforcing a status hierarchy in world order. Only Washington and Moscow went to strategic arms control meetings. Beijing, Paris, London and Delhi weren't invited to this party. This institutionalised the world order into a two-tiered system: the superpowers and all the rest.

Given that there are many ways to use nuclear weapons, when these are considered it seems difficult to accept the naive theory that a new major power rivalry won't also be a nuclear one. Deterrence is only one criterion. It was the most important criterion in the first nuclear age, and probably will be in the second. But it is still only one criterion. Frühling's essay gives several examples of this very point. If Australia gets the bomb, so might Indonesia, and this would be bad for arms control and stability. Another example: Chinese precision attacks on Canberra and American bases could be used to punish Australia for cooperating with the United States. We are beyond deterrence in both examples.

We can stipulate that we don't want to enter this world of the unthinkable. That's easy. But it doesn't mean that we *won't* enter it. In fact, North Korea's growing arsenal shows that we already have, whether anyone likes to say so or not. Add Pakistan and Israel – and the modernisation of the US, Russian and Chinese nuclear arsenals as well. I would cite the virtual collapse of serious arms control thinking at the moment as another sign that a second nuclear age is well underway.

As for Australia and the bomb, it's useful to recall the tagline Herman Kahn gave to his work in the 1960s. It was "thinking *about* the unthinkable" – not "thinking the unthinkable". There's a huge difference between the two. Few problems are better dealt with by *not* thinking about them, as it only invites intuitive decision-making. There are a lot of examples of such decision-making these days. The choice about nuclear posture shouldn't be one of them.

Paul Bracken, professor of political science
and management at Yale University

Stephan Frühling responds

I am grateful for Alison Broinowski's and Paul Bracken's thoughtful comments on my article, "A Nuclear-armed Australia". They approach their responses from what seem at first very different angles: in Broinowski's case, the history and arguments that have sustained the strong public support for nuclear disarmament in Australia; in Bracken's, the role of nuclear weapons in future relations between the great powers. But the common theme underlying both responses is the shape of the future international "nuclear order" – the strategic environment within which Australia will have to develop its policy towards nuclear weapons.

Australia's historical support for non-proliferation was rooted in a clear-eyed analysis of our strategic circumstances and the benefit of keeping nuclear weapons from our neighbourhood – a point made very clearly in then foreign minister Gareth Evans' statement on Australia's regional security in 1989, for example. This is still an important consideration against Australian nuclear proliferation, and it is an argument that should fare much better in the face of geostrategic change than the ideational aspirations that have come to dominate the non-proliferation movement in recent years – a fact that makes the significant reduction in Australian government funding for regional non-proliferation efforts over the last twenty years all the more deplorable.

Broinowski writes that the term "order" "hardly applies to today's disorderly world". Yet many of her arguments rest on the assumption that crucial elements of the international order of the last forty years – which saw strong US and Soviet support for the Non-Proliferation Treaty (NPT) during the Cold War, and from the wider international community after the 1991 Gulf War – will endure. For example, she seems certain that the international community would impose sanctions on Australia if it exercised its right to leave the NPT – even though, as I argued in my article, Australia would clearly not take such a step against US opposition. Nor does she seem to concede the possibility that Australia may in future need to raise defence spending to levels where developing nuclear weapons would not be "crippling" – although it should be pointed out that Israel, Pakistan, India, China, South Africa and North Korea all demonstrated that acquiring nuclear weapons is "feasible" even with economies that were, at the time of acquisition, much smaller than Australia's today.

If Australia saw no need to raise its defence spending, and the international community, including the United States, remained cohesive and willing to bear the cost of preventing proliferation, Australia would indeed not be on a trajectory towards the acquisition of nuclear weapons. The question, however, is will the current "disorder" revert to this order? The international (and nuclear) order of the last half-century was benign for Australia, as an Anglo-Saxon outpost on the edge of an Asia dominated by the United States. This makes the prospect that it is now ending particularly agonising. But it only reinforces Australian governments' responsibility to assess how long-standing judgements about our security, and the role of nuclear weapons, may need to change as our strategic environment does.

It would be too far-fetched to predict that Australia will, should or even could acquire nuclear weapons. But it is equally wrong to assume that it shouldn't, couldn't or wouldn't, for, as Paul Bracken points out, international politics and technology suggest that their role will remain "substantial" in future rivalries between major powers. He cautions against the assumption that the only purpose of nuclear weapons is to counteract those of rivals. Such a proposition is attractive to those who see the main task of nuclear policy as pursuing (if necessary, unilateral) disarmament, yet it is ahistorical and inconsistent with the way nuclear weapons are "used" by great powers today.

Nuclear coercion currently plays less of a role for China than for Russia, which is developing the capabilities, doctrine and approach of openly threatening early but limited use of nuclear weapons to win a regional conflict. The prospective end of the Intermediate-Range Nuclear Forces Treaty, which all NATO allies now agree Russia is openly violating, is likely to reinforce the role that nuclear weapons can play in the Western response to Russia's reintroduction of this class of missiles. As Bracken points out, the "use" of nuclear weapons includes general deterrence; shaping adversary behaviour in times of crises, through threats as well as use; and influencing adversaries' defence investment – and, one might add, the management of relations between the United States and its allies. Since the beginning of the atomic age, great and not-so-great powers have relied on nuclear weapons to address threats from other states that they thought could not be managed by their conventional forces. But the Cold War stayed cold, and no country saw it necessary to actually use nuclear weapons in anger, attesting to the degree of caution that they introduce into world affairs.

There is no doubt a great danger in rushing into nuclear proliferation. Yet, as Bracken remarks, there is also danger in taboos. One of the great tragedies of the twentieth century is that liberal democracies clung to the hope that if they demonstrated their good intent by eschewing the means to deter attack, they could preserve the peace and the order that they valued so much, while author- itarian powers underestimated the ultimate willingness of liberal democracies to fight for their sovereignty and survival. Broinowski concludes her response by writing, "A country whose leaders can force others to suffer 'what they must' ... should first consider treating others as they wish to be treated." This, indeed, is perhaps the most crucial conclusion to be drawn from an argument that even Australia might, under some circumstances, decide to seek security through nuclear weapons. For if the great powers of Asia don't heed this warning, other countries in the region – including Australia – do have options to defend themselves and their sovereignty, unpalatable as they may be.

Stephan Frühling, associate professor in the Strategic and Defence Studies Centre of the Australian National University

Subscribe to Australian Foreign Affairs & save up to 28% on the cover price.

Enjoy free home delivery of the print edition and full digital access to the journal via the Australian Foreign Affairs website, iPad, iPhone and Android apps.

Forthcoming issue:
Our Sphere of Influence:
Rivalry in the Pacific (July 2019)

Never miss an issue. Subscribe and save.

☐ **1 year auto-renewing print and digital subscription** (3 issues) $49.99 within Australia. Outside Australia $79.99*

☐ **1 year print and digital subscription** (3 issues) $59.99 within Australia. Outside Australia $99.99

☐ **1 year auto-renewing digital subscription** (3 issues) $29.99.*

☐ **2 year print and digital subscription** (6 issues) $114.99 within Australia.

☐ Tick here to commence subscription with the current issue.

Give an inspired gift. Subscribe a friend.

☐ **1 year print and digital gift subscription** (3 issues) $59.99 within Australia. Outside Australia $99.99

☐ **1 year digital-only gift subscription** (3 issues) $29.99.

☐ **2 year print and digital gift subscription** (6 issues) $114.99 within Australia.

☐ Tick here to commence subscription with the current issue.

ALL PRICES INCLUDE GST, POSTAGE AND HANDLING.

*Your subscription will automatically renew until you notify us to stop. Prior to the end of your subscription period, we will send you a reminder notice.

Please turn over for subscription order form, or subscribe online at **australianforeignaffairs.com**
Alternatively, call 1800 077 514 or +61 3 9486 0288 or email **subscribe@australianforeignaffairs.com**

Back Issues ALL PRICES INCLUDE GST, POSTAGE AND HANDLING.

☐ **AFA2** ($22.99)
Trump in Asia

☐ **AFA3** ($22.99)
Australia & Indonesia

☐ **AFA4** ($22.99)
Defending Australia

PAYMENT DETAILS I enclose a cheque/money order made out to Schwartz Publishing Pty Ltd.
Or please debit my credit card (MasterCard, Visa or Amex accepted).

CARD NO. ☐☐☐☐ ☐☐☐☐ ☐☐☐☐ ☐☐☐☐

EXPIRY DATE   /   CCV   AMOUNT $

CARDHOLDER'S NAME

SIGNATURE

NAME

ADDRESS

EMAIL   PHONE

Post or fax this form to: Reply Paid 90094, Carlton VIC 3053 **Freecall:** 1800 077 514 **or** +61 3 9486 0288
Fax: (03) 9011 6106 **Email:** subscribe@australianforeignaffairs.com **Website:** australianforeignaffairs.com
Subscribe online at australianforeignaffairs.com/subscribe

In 2019, we are delighted to announce Next Voices.
Until Sunday, 10 March, we are open for submissions
on the topic of this issue, *Are We Asian Yet?*
History vs Geography, to publish on the
Australian Foreign Affairs website.

NEXT VOICES

The best new thinkers on Australian foreign affairs

Contributions must be 1500–2000 words and previously unpublished. Authors whose work is selected will receive AU$100 and a one-year print and digital subscription to Australian Foreign Affairs, and will collaborate with Australian Foreign Affairs editors to shape and refine their piece.

Writers do not have to be foreign-affairs experts: journalists, academics, foreign-aid workers, policy advisers, students and other interested readers are encouraged to submit. We hope to foster and promote a diverse stable of writers from Australia and the Asia-Pacific, and to encourage discussion on foreign affairs that represents a range of views in the broader Australian community.

To read our guidelines and submit,
visit **australianforeignaffairs.com/next-voices**

The Back Page

THE FRIEDMAN UNIT

What is it: A time period equivalent to "the next six months"; also known as an FU or a Friedman.

Who coined it: Duncan Black (blogger, *Eschaton*), in 2006, in response to Thomas Friedman (columnist, *New York Times*) repeatedly declaring that "the next six months" was a critical period in the Iraq War. Friedman made similar statements on fourteen occasions in three years.

Who bought it: Much of Washington. In the pre-Trump era, Friedman was, according to Robert M. Entman (professor, George Washington University), "probably the most influential foreign affairs columnist in American journalism". Frank Rich (writer, *New York Magazine*) listed Friedman among the "liberal hawks" who promoted the Iraq War and US "neo-isolationism".

What happened to it: Friedman was interviewed in 2007 by Stephen Colbert (host, *The Colbert Report*), who pointed out the timeline of overlapping FUs. The columnist agreed to stop using the phrase, saying, "I'm afraid we've run out of six months. It's really time to set a deadline." He subsequently urged Barack Obama (former president, United States) to extend the troop withdrawal until 2011; pundits suggested this was another FU.

Further reading: Friedman has coined other phrases, including "The first rule of holes is when you're in one, stop digging. When you're in three, bring a lot of shovels" and "The only engine big enough to impact Mother Nature is Father Greed".

What happened to Thomas Friedman: He remains a *New York Times* columnist, reportedly with a "near unlimited expense account".